organic
superfoods

orga

super

nic
foods

michael van straten

mitchell beazley

Dedication

This book is dedicated to my first grandson, Jamie,
in the hope that he will grow up stronger and healthier
thanks to organic superfoods. And to my children,
Sacha and Tanya, who, despite their initial resistance
to anything remotely healthy as children, have come to
enjoy organic food and the benefits it can bring.
MvS

Organic Superfoods
by Michael van Straten

Organic Superfoods is meant to be used as a general
reference and recipe book. While the author believes
the information and recipes it contains are beneficial
to health, the book is in no way intended to replace
medical advice. You are therefore urged to consult
your health-care professional about specific medical
complaints and the use of healing herbs and foods
in the treatment thereof.

First published in Great Britain in 1999
by Mitchell Beazley, an imprint of
Octopus Publishing Group Limited,
2–4 Heron Quays, London E14 4JP.
Reprinted 2000

While all reasonable care has been taken during
the preparation of this edition, neither the publisher,
editors, nor the author can accept responsibility
for any consequences arising from the use thereof or
from the information contained herein.

ISBN 1840002069

A CIP catalogue record for this book is available from
the British Library.

Commissioning Editor: Margaret Little
Art Director: Gaye Allen
Executive Art Editor: Tracy Killick
Design: Miranda Harvey
Editor: Jamie Ambrose
Editorial Assistant: Stephen Guise
Production: Karen Farquhar
Index: Ann Barrett

Typeset in M Baskerville, Simoncini Garamond
and Vectora
Printed and bound by Toppan Printing Company
in China

contents

why
org

go

anic?

what is organic and why choose it?

During the late 1950s, I abandoned my plans to study conventional medicine and became a student at the British College of Naturopathy and Osteopathy. Even in those days, the risks of the increasing chemical pollution of our food and the environment were being discussed at college – and that is when my involvement with organically grown food first began. It seemed so obvious that chemicals strong enough to kill weeds, poison insects and destroy fungal infections must also have some form of detrimental effect on the human body, not to mention the living world around us.

Forty years later, people are waking up to the alarms that have been ignored for so long, and organic food is no longer the preserve of the beards-and-sandals brigade. Today, virtually every British supermarket stocks some form of organic produce; the biggest take-away pizza company in the UK has banned genetically modified foods; and organic home-delivery schemes are not just thriving but multiplying. "Organic" has become the buzz-word of the new millennium.

Healthy food for balanced living

Organic farming and horticulture and domestic organic gardening produce healthy animals, untainted food and the freshest, healthiest produce. Why? The reason is simple: organically reared animals and organically grown fruits and vegetables ideally harbour no artificial fertilisers and none of the hundreds of legally permitted insecticides, pesticides, fungicides, herbicides, waxes, hormones, antibiotics or other additives present in non-organic foodstuffs. I say "ideally" because even organically maintained farms are susceptible to "background pollution" (from residues already present in water, soil and air) and pesticide drift from neighbouring non-organic farms. Yet even with these problems, the produce from organic farms is still a healthier, safer choice for you and your family. Unlike soil that has suffered chemical abuse, organically maintained soil is rich and well balanced, full of the worms, micro-organisms and friendly bacteria nature intended it to have. It carries no poisons to leach into streams and rivers because creatures that would otherwise destroy food crops are kept in check by natural predators.

Soil benefits are only the beginning. Just like human beings, a well-fed, cared for and naturally reared plant has a stronger resistance to infections and a better ability to withstand climatic stresses. More importantly from the consumer's point of view, it will (if properly harvested, transported and stored) contain a greater amount of essential nutrients – not to mention flavour – when it is allowed to ripen naturally and is eaten in peak condition.

Further along the food-supply chain, all manufactured foods that carry the organic symbol must, by law, be produced according to rigorous standards which do not allow the addition of artificial colourings, flavourings, preservatives, or flavour enhancers. Thus, they will contain no tartrazine to give your children asthma, no monosodium glutamate to give you a headache.

While controlling the food we eat is an important line of defence in the war against chemicals, it is, unfortunately, not enough in itself. Agricultural chemicals (agrochemicals) are also found in the water we drink. Many fertilisers and other agrochemicals leach from non-organic farmland into the underground water table, streams, rivers and reservoirs, and they inevitably come out of the tap. By choosing an organic diet, however, you at least reduce the pollutants in your body – which makes you better able to cope with those you can't control.

Ten good reasons

The Soil Association, a UK-based registered charity and organic certifying body that promotes better understanding of the links between organic agriculture, the environment and human health, lists ten reasons why we should all go organic:

1 to protect future generations;
2 to pay the real cost of real food;
3 to have an independent guarantee;
4 to protect water quality;
5 to enjoy greater flavour and nutrition;
6 to keep chemicals off your plate;
7 to reduce global warming and save energy;
8 to prevent soil erosion;
9 to help small farmers; and
10 to help restore biodiversity.

In the UK, more than 25,000 tons of agrochemicals are spread on the land each year. Even more frighteningly, in the US, the figure is almost *four million tons* – an amount that represents an almost 30-fold increase since the end of the Second World War. It is extraordinary that, despite the warnings issued by Rachel Carson in her classic book *Silent Spring*, first published in 1962, it has taken until the millennium for the general public to sit up and take notice. Unfortunately for us and the environment, many governments have yet to do so.

benefits of an organic lifestyle

Flavour

Try an organic taste-test. Close your eyes and take a bite of an organic apple, then take a bite from a commercially grown one. Or dip your organic wholemeal bread soldier, made from stone-ground, organically grown wheat, into the yolk of an organic free-range egg, and compare that with a finger of white, sliced, commercial blunderloaf dipped into the pale, anaemic yolk of a battery-farmed egg. You won't need a degree in food technology to tell which one tastes better.

If you're a meat-eater, compare organic, chemical-free sausages and bacon, or roast rib of organic English beef with a factory-farmed, commercially produced, non-organic equivalent. For the majority of people – including most of the great chefs – organic *anything* wins hands down, primarily because of its full, rich, natural flavours and superb textures, but also, of course, because organic beef is free from BSE.

Animal welfare

None of us should avoid responsibility for animal welfare, and if we buy meat taken from organically reared animals, we are taking a step in the right direction. Organic standards for animal welfare are generally higher than those of other types of welfare-conscious label, including free range. To qualify for any of the recognised organic symbols, it isn't enough for farmers to avoid chemicals; the animals in their care must also live natural, contented lives. Chickens must be free-range. Pigs must be allowed to give birth to their piglets naturally, in proper sties with plenty of room. Calves must be allowed to suckle from their mothers.

Protecting the environment

Every time you purchase an organic product, you help reduce global warming by saving the energy used to produce agrochemicals. You're also protecting the biodiversity of our planet by not killing beneficial organisms: plants as well as insects, birds and small mammals. Britain has lost thousands of miles of ancient hedges, nearly all of its traditional flower meadows and huge numbers of once common songbirds as well as birds of prey thanks to today's intensive-farming methods. By simply planting an organic garden, you redress part of the balance.

Nutrition

Without doubt, organically produced crops are richer in nutrients than their commercially grown counterparts. The organic farmer uses traditional methods such as crop rotation, green manure, composting and organic fertilisers to keep the soil in good health and to replace nutrients taken up by previous crops. Intensive commercial cultivation, on the other hand, relies on artificial fertilisers that replace only the nutrients essential to grow the plants, with scant regard to their all-round nutritional quality. Similarly, intensive livestock producers have to use feed supplemented with minerals and vitamins to replace those missing from their own non-organic feed crops. Non-organic produce tends to have a much higher water content, and thus contains fewer essential vitamins and minerals – which is why studies show consistently higher levels of vitamins A and C in organic fruits and vegetables.

In the mountain of current food legislation (which, in itself, has used up several forests in the printing process), laws cover everything from seeds to packaging, storage to handling, dairy and shop hygiene, sell-by dates to labelling... even the size and shape of bananas! Yet nowhere is there a law that makes testing for nutritional quality obligatory.

Human health

A recent Danish study of farmers running organic farms found that their sperm count was double that of the average traditional farmer. Whether this is due to eating organic food or the result of avoiding agrochemicals isn't certain, but either way, the results are sobering. It doesn't matter whether you choose it for taste, for safety, or in order to protect the environment. It doesn't matter whether you can switch to a completely organic diet. Every organic product you consume is better for *your* health and better for the planet. But if you're pregnant or thinking of it, feeding young children, or suffering or recovering from serious illness, then it is even more vital that you make organic food as big a part of your regular shopping list as you can possibly afford.

Quality of life

A recent Soil Association survey revealed two unexpected benefits of growing organic produce in addition to the benefits of avoiding exposure to a multitude of chemicals. It found that people who started to use their certified organic home-delivery box schemes returned to traditional cooking after years of freezer-to-microwave dishes. Secondly, once the chief cook went to the trouble of cooking traditional meals, he or she started to insist on traditional meal times. All over the country, families reported that they were sitting down to eat together for the first time in ages.

risks of a non-organic lifestyle

Serious health and safety issues surround the amount of agrochemicals already present in the food chain and the environment at large. Consider just a few of the facts:

● Excessive amounts of nitrate fertilisers have infiltrated many of our water supplies, making them unsafe for babies. Even the British government – slow to act at the best of times – has warned consumers to cut the tops and tails off carrots and peel them before use, due to the risk of chemical contamination.

● Milk has been contaminated with antibiotics, DDT and, most recently, lindane. Lindane, an organochlorine, appears to have strong links with the causes of breast cancer; it is already banned or very restricted in nearly 40 countries, yet seeds are still being treated with this toxic chemical and certain crops may be sprayed with it as much as four times.

● UK government studies continue to demonstrate the presence of lindane in a range of imported fruits, vegetables, grains, meat, dairy products and even baby milk. A third of all animal foods tested in the UK were also found to contain this highly toxic pesticide. Is it coincidence that 40 per cent more cases of breast cancer occur in Lincolnshire – where one of the main crops is sugar beet, a crop sprayed with lindane – than in the rest of the UK?

Chemical roulette

The situation is not just a European problem. Even in a country such as the US, which prides itself on setting standards for consumer protection, statistics make very grim reading. For example, the US Environmental Protection Agency published a 14-page list of pesticides known to cause cancer in humans, or else to be probable or possible causes. It classifies these chemicals under headings such as "Cannot be determined but suggestive", "Probable human carcinogens with limited human evidence", "Probable human carcinogens with sufficient evidence in animals", and most frighteningly, "Human carcinogens".

In an effort to find out exactly what was being poured onto food and, ultimately, into the average human body, the US Consumer's Union analysed the US Department of Agriculture's own pesticide data on 27,000 food samples, devising a computer-created toxicity index (or TI) for each food. The higher the TI number, the greater the amount of pesticide contained, and therefore the greater the toxicity level. Consistently on top of the chemical table were American-grown peaches, green beans and winter squash, and domestic and imported apples, grapes, spinach and pears, all with TI scores around ten times higher than other produce with unacceptably high scores. Yet society has not learned from such information. Ten years after the US banned a cancer-causing pesticide called alar, which was widely used on apples, the country's use of highly cancerous fungicides and neuro-toxic organophosphates has doubled – despite the fact that the land area devoted to apple orchards has decreased considerably.

Trading in toxins

When produce is imported from developing countries, controls on the use of agrochemicals are even more doubtful – more so when you learn that agrochemicals outlawed in developed countries are shipped to them on a regular basis. Large quantities of fashionable miniature vegetables come from these countries. Because such vegetables have a larger surface area, they absorb more chemicals by weight than mature vegetables, and pose even higher risks.

Chemical contamination has also been found in strawberries, peppers, peaches, melon, apples, apricots and grapes imported from Chile. Fungicides are widely used on citrus fruits in many countries, and are often sprayed on out-of-season vegetables. As if that weren't enough, illegal growth-promoting agents have been detected in meat samples throughout Europe as well as in the UK. Which brings us to the question of antibiotics.

Rise of the superbugs

Widely used legally in animal feeds as growth-promoting agents (and probably in wider use illegally), antibiotics are causing resistant strains of bacteria to develop in animals, including some farmed fish. If humans become infected with these organisms, conventional antibiotic treatment may not be enough. The relentless drip of such antibiotics into the food chain, coupled with years of over-prescription by careless doctors, means that we could soon face a spate of life-threatening "superbugs". Drastic action is required to remove these compounds from agriculture, where they're used only for commercial gain. As organic meat, poultry, eggs and dairy products are certain to be free of antibiotics, the choice for the consumer is clear.

The organic solution

The term "organic" doesn't just relate to the way in which food is grown, farmed and produced; it also includes what happens to food throughout every stage of the manufacturing process. Going organic is your only guarantee of avoiding the vast range of added chemicals used in the food-processing industry throughout the world.

additives
and flavourings

Over the last few years, enormous media coverage has been given to the subject of food allergies. We've read about people suffering from "total allergy syndrome": being allergic not only to many additives used in food processing, but also to the world we live in, including its food and polluted air and water. While there are some very specific allergic reactions to individual foods – particularly nuts, shellfish, eggs, milk and strawberries – the majority of people who develop side effects from foods do not suffer from allergies. They *do* suffer, but their conditions are more accurately described as adverse food reactions, or food intolerance.

Additives mean added risk

For the population at large, and for children in particular, my major concern is the ever-increasing exposure to food additives such as preservatives, artificial colourings and flavours, flavour enhancers, and artificial sweeteners. Any of these may cause reactions such as asthma, skin problems and dramatic behavioural changes in children. What's even more worrying is that few are known to be completely safe, and some are believed to cause cancer in laboratory animals.

One great advantage of choosing organic produce is that you avoid the dreaded "E numbers", first brought to the public's attention by Maurice Hanssen in his revolutionary book *E for Additives* (Thorsons Publishing, 1986). Admittedly, some are safe, natural substances such as vitamins B_2, C and E, saffron and lecithin. Most, however, are best avoided. This, of course, is easier said than done, as the selection in the table opposite shows. If you've just eaten a slice of typical commercial Swiss roll, you might have consumed all the additives in this list. Imagine what could happen if a food-sensitive child ate one.

The organic alternative

Going organic is the only sure way of avoiding chemical additives such as these. It is also the safest way for you and your family to avoid coming down with any "allergy" in the future.

E no.	name	description	found in	adverse effects
E440a	Liquid pectin	Stabiliser and emulsifier	Yoghurts, jams, jellies and confectionery	May cause stomach distension and flatulence
E465	Ethylmethyl-cellulose	Stabiliser and emulsifier	Ice-cream, bakery goods, packet soups and sauces	May cause bloating and flatulence
E471	Mono-diglyceride	Stabiliser and emulsifier	Cake fillings, cream biscuits and salad dressings	No known side effects
E330	Citric acid	Antioxidant that prevents discolouration	A wide range of foods and beverages	Large quantities can damage tooth enamel
E102	Tartrazine	Yellow colouring agent	In squashes and other beverage items, fish fingers, breadcrumbs, cakes, canned peas and some medicines	Seriously affects food-sensitive children, causing blurred vision, sleeplessness, hyperactivity, skin rashes. Particularly strong irritant for asthmatics or aspirin-sensitive people
E110	Sunset yellow	Yellow colouring agent	Fish cakes, sauces, packet soups, cakes, biscuits and some medicines	Irritant for hyperactive children. Can produce allergies in adults, especially skin rashes and stomach problems in those with aspirin sensitivity
E123	Amaranth	Red colouring agent	Fruit pies, canned pie fillings, yoghurts and jam	Causes rashes in people with aspirin sensitivity; enhances hyperactivity in children
E124	Ponceau 4R	Red colouring agent	Glacé cherries, canned fruits, packet soups and pork pies	Can affect asthmatics and hyperactive children
E202	Potassium sorbate	Preservative	Dairy products, cooked/cured meats, meat pies and pâtés	No known side effects
E282	Calcium propionate	Preservative	Bread	No known side effects

GM foods: what are the real risks?

Genetic engineering has been heralded as one of the great scientific advances of the late 20th century. It holds the promise of preventing genetically inherited diseases as well as of finding a cure for people already afflicted with some of the worst of these conditions. But then came Dolly, the cloned sheep, and genetic engineering moved from the sheltered cloisters of medical research into the open forum of public morality. Would mad scientists unleash Frankenstein-like monsters? Would a new Hitler emerge, a dictator who would set about creating the ultimate genetically pure master race?

A recent addition to this list of anxieties are genetically modified, or GM, foods. Yet would these really be such a disaster, especially considering that botanists, horticulturists, farmers and animal breeders have been messing about with genes for hundreds of years? Even when we choose a partner, we are making a conscious decision to "genetically engineer" our offspring. We've already created "early" and "late" varieties of food crops; plants with a stronger natural resistance to disease and insects; pigs with less fat for leaner bacon; chickens which lay an egg every day; cattle that produce more milk; turkeys that are ready for butchering in less time and thus require less food. Man has tampered with the genetic structure of our environment for centuries, so what is so different about the contemporary biotechnology that allows scientists to manipulate genes in a laboratory?

Human guinea pigs

The answer is that the "laboratory" these food scientists are using covers the entire earth, and among the guinea pigs in this experiment are human beings – in many cases, human beings who don't even realise they're being treated as experimental animals. Thanks to the huge ground swell of opposition and the growing public fears about these so-called "Frankenstein foods", however, the situation is changing day by day – hopefully for the better.

As far as attitudes in the UK toward this subject are concerned, a real spanner was thrown in the works when Professor Arpad Pusztai blew the whistle on experiments he was conducting at the Rowett Institute in Aberdeen, Scotland. According to the professor, rats fed with GM potatoes developed smaller internal organs and poor-quality immune systems compared to rats fed on normal potatoes. Pusztai's statement proved a powerful weapon for concerned groups such as the Soil Association, Friends of the Earth, English Nature, and all of the other organisations already campaigning against the spread of GM foods.

Meanwhile, in the US, the waters had already been muddied by allowing genetically modified soya beans to be mixed with conventional beans at source, which resulted in there being no way of separating the two. Obviously aware that, given the choice, many consumers would prefer to avoid the GM beans altogether, the soya-bean producers decided to make such a choice impossible.

Hidden concerns

At present, the soya bean is probably the foodstuff most at risk of genetic modification. Around one-third of the total American production is already genetically modified; when you realise that ingredients such as soya-bean oil, soya lecithin and soya flour are found in around two-thirds of all manufactured foods, the picture is fairly gloomy indeed. According to Friends of the Earth, maize (corn) is the next crop most likely to appear in a GM version on supermarket shelves, and more fruits and vegetables are due to follow. Given that very few of these ingredients are labelled as being genetically modified, it is impossible to tell whether or not you are actually buying them.

Want to worry some more? Then take a look around your own kitchen. Canned meat products, frozen pizzas, instant soups, sauces, curries, baby foods, cereals, pasta, bread and biscuits, baby milk, snacks, ice-cream, chocolate, veggie-burgers, soya milk, even pet food... all these and more are likely to contain some form of genetically modified ingredient.

Transplanting trouble

Unlike traditional selective breeding, genetic engineering often involves physically removing genes from one species and putting them into another – in some cases, from plants into animals, and vice versa. Companies funding such research claim it is being done in an effort to feed the world, but at the end of the day, it's actually to line their pockets.

So what are the risks? Take the example of herbicide-resistant soya beans. What they are designed to resist is a herbicide called Round-up®. This means that crops previously not sprayed with this toxic, non-biodegradable herbicide can now be sprayed with impunity – which will lead to higher residues in the crops and a greater risk of traces entering the food chain. This, of course, is completely contrary to the GM manufacturing firms' claims that genetic alteration will result in fewer chemicals being poured into the earth; in fact, it is entirely possible that even more will be used than ever before.

Gone with the wind?

As yet, there is no guarantee that genetically engineered resistance to bacteria and viruses, in both plants and animals, will not spread into the microbial community at large, producing even more strains of antibiotic-resistant organisms, some of which could well infect humans. There is also the risk that insects and weeds will become resistant to existing herbicides – with the result that even more dangerous chemicals will be sprayed on our food to combat them.

In the UK, there are already some 300 government-approved sites on farms where test plantings of GM strawberries, potatoes and oilseed rape are being conducted, and there are serious concerns about the way in which these sites are being run and monitored. One prosecution has already taken place because of a failure to leave sufficient space around the GM plantings; many experts believe that this officially designated "buffer zone" is far too small in any case. Wind-borne pollen and bees can travel considerable distances, and there is already evidence that some genetically altered plants have enhanced reproductive properties, which could lead to much easier cross-pollination with non-GM crops.

In the US, the Environmental Protection Agency suspects that any predators that are repelled or damaged by genetically engineered resistant crops will themselves build up an immunity to those genetic changes. Three to four years is the time span that is predicted before these new "genetically engineered" pests would evolve, creating a need for new variants or stronger insecticides and pesticides to control them.

Doomed bees and terminator traps

Bees, the lifeline of the food chain, are heavily at risk from genetic meddling. Test fields of oilseed rape, bred to produce its own insecticide, are already killing off bees as well as predatory insects. If this insecticidal gene escaped into the plant community at large, it wouldn't be long before no bees were left to pollinate fruit trees or other flowering plants.

Further alarms are being raised by what the genetic modifiers themselves call "terminator technology", which ensures that some GM seeds can be used only for one crop; afterwards, any seeds will be infertile. Besides purchasing more of these GM seeds from the same source, you might well have to buy the company's agrochemicals, too, as part of a package. Not surprisingly, the Soil Association is alarmed by such future prospects.

According to director Patrick Holden, "The five major agrochemical companies envisage a future where only a handful of varieties of wheat, maize, rice and other food crops are grown commercially. They are working flat out now to ensure that, within a decade, most of the world's staple crops will be [derived] from genetically modified seeds – which they have engineered." What, then, will happen to biodiversity? What will happen to our wildlife?

A number of government agencies are concerned about these risks and have called for a halt on further plantings until more research has been conducted. English Nature, in particular, is complaining about the environmentally untested introduction of genetically engineered crops that could spell disaster for the linnet, the skylark and the corn bunting if the wild plants, seeds and insects on which they feed vanish from our farm lands. The group's supporters are urging the government to proceed with caution.

The battle for safety

Thankfully, they are not alone. Some of England's leading scientists, food writers and health experts have joined the battle against this vast commercial exploitation. Prince Charles himself has spoken out passionately against it. Schools throughout the country have banned GM foods; they are even prohibited in the kitchens of the House of Commons – yet ministers behave just as they did over the salmonella fiasco of the late 1980s and the BSE disaster.

Indeed, there is more than a little confusion in Downing Street. Science minister Lord Sainsbury appeared to support a three-year moratorium on the commercial growing of GM crops. Following his comments, an official ministerial spokesman and Environment Minister Michael Meacher each declared on television that the government had no such plans. A government document leaked to Friends of the Earth suggested otherwise: it flatly contradicted the verbal denials and laid out plans to extend the voluntary one-year moratorium to three years, yet it also admits that even this won't be long enough to determine the environmental impact of the farm-based trials.

Public pressure

If this sounds too apocalyptic, then take heart. The disgraceful saga of salmonella in our chickens and eggs, BSE in our cattle and CJD in our population has a silver lining. These three events have done for food what the thalidomide tragedy did for medicine: made people aware that governments, scientists and industry are fallible and their pursuit of profit is often at an unacceptable cost to people and the planet. GM foods are the last straw, and the British public, at least, is voting with its purse by turning away from non-organic food. When supermarkets announce they've contracted to buy the entire production of the organic milk cooperative for the next five years, and when one after another they renounce the use of GM foods in their own-label products, we know the tide is turning.

industrial agriculture versus organic farming

Any discussion of the relative merits of industrial agriculture versus organic farming must look at three interrelated factors: energy costs, environmental damage and the health risk-and-benefit equation.

The energy equation

Proponents of vast agribusiness enterprises claim that their super-efficiency, massive yields per acre and uniformity of produce is the only way to feed the world. While it is generally true that organic methods of production result in smaller yields per acre, the overall energy costs of coming up with the final product are a fraction of those of their industrialised counterparts.

Enormous quantities of fossil fuels are used in the production of agrochemicals. Energy is needed for the manufacture of their basic ingredients; for collection, delivery and conversion into finished products; for their distribution and for multiple applications by the end user. Such is the imbalance that calculations show a thousand calories of fuel expenditure for every hundred calories worth of food produced. It goes without saying that the combustion of these negative calories adds enormously to global warming and atmospheric pollution. For example, non-organic farming in the US uses more oil – to make and apply synthetic fertilisers, herbicides, pesticides and insecticides – than any other industry in that country.

On the other hand, the organic farmer relies on more manpower, creating employment in rural areas where there is often little other work available. The fossil-fuel requirements of organic farming are significantly lower because organic methods involve no applications of insecticides, herbicides, pesticides and synthetic fertilisers.

Environmental time bombs

The high levels of energy used by industrialised agriculture do enormous damage to our environment. Almost more worrying, however, is the potential for environmental disaster that results from the toxic time bomb of highly dangerous substances accumulating steadily in our soil and water. Monocropping – growing only one type of wheat, rye, etc – and increasing applications of synthetic fertilisers are destroying the soil. What many people don't realise is that soil is a living thing, rich in humus that gives it structure and organic matter that fills it with nutrients to nourish not only the crops we eat, but the animals that feed off those crops, which in turn produce milk, eggs, cheese, butter and meat for us to eat, too. Our entire ecosystem is a delicate balancing act; once that balance is destroyed, nature is disrupted. Insects, worms, caterpillars, rodents, birds, wildflowers and even beneficial bacteria vanish. We destroy one pest with chemicals only to find that a worse pest that it fed on now does more damage to our crops. Kill the ladybirds, and greenfly inherit your garden.

The key to our survival on this planet is a sustained maintenance of biodiversity. We must preserve the gene bank of thousands of varieties of food plants and we must protect the as-yet-undiscovered medicinal plants that could hold the key to the treatment of cancer, AIDS and other life-threatening diseases. During my visits to the Brazilian rainforest, I have seen at first hand the results of deforestation and indiscriminate use of herbicides and pesticides on vast tracts of virgin forest. Ethnobotanist Professor Walter Accorsi took me to some of the worst areas and pointed out that, by the millennium, man will have destroyed 25,000 plant species, many of them still unknown and uninvestigated. Statistically, 200 of them are likely to have extremely important medicinal uses.

Direct health risks

The cost of industrial agriculture doesn't stop at plants; for example, nitrates leach from the soil into the water supply. In fact, so many agrochemicals end up in our water that, in heavily farmed regions, local water authorities spend tens of millions of pounds on special treatment plants – and those treatments don't prevent all chemicals from reaching our tap water.

Pollution of our air, land and water, as well as of our food, is a major hazard to the health of this planet and its people. It is only avoidable by following organic practices – which are also the only way to protect human health from the dreadful hazards of intensive farming. The link between the pesticide lindane and breast cancer, for example, is so well established that why this deadly chemical has not been banned remians a mystery, yet it is often used to control leatherjackets and wireworm. Organic farmers, meanwhile, encourage birds and beetles to feed on these pests, and use crop rotation schemes to reduce their numbers.

The cruel irony of intensive farming is that farmers are often the worst victims of agrochemicals; neurological illnesses caused by exposure to organophosphate sheep dip have the most severe consequences. And farmers are not solely to blame. Many of the most toxic chemicals are used by domestic gardeners, on golf courses, sports fields and public gardens – areas in which there is no excuse for anything but organic practices. We are already paying the price for going down the non-organic road. It will only get higher the farther we travel.

There are a number of reasons why people choose organic produce over conventional, commercially produced food. While there is no doubt that organic food wins hands down every time for taste – just ask any top chef, or, even better, try a taste test for yourself – and that this is an important consideration for many, it is by no means the most significant. If you decide to grow your own organic produce, you will also know that your garden shed or allotment is a safe place for your children. No toxic chemicals, no risk of horrifying accidents

the organic

and no chance of harming your pets either. On a global scale there are major and incremental benefits that go along with the increasing acreage of organic farming: a reduced consumption of agrochemicals and a consequent reduction in the use of fossil fuels needed for their manufacture, distribution and application. Less energy consumption means less global warming, less environmental damage, less of a contribution to the greenhouse effect and the vital protection of biodiversity.

The real beauty of organic food, however, is that not only is it naturally delicious and environmentally friendly, but that it also makes an invaluable contribution to your health. The medicinal benefits of going organic, however, are something that only a few people fully appreciate.

OUT OF HARM'S WAY Many of my patients, especially those with young families, tell me that they prefer organic produce because they know it protects their children from the potential hazards posed by the huge range of pesticides, insecticides, herbicides, anti-fungals and after-harvest chemicals that are poured so liberally onto most commercial crops. Avoiding these dangers, although reason enough for anyone, young or old, is only part of the story: going organic is not just a question of protecting yourself and your family, but also one of positive gain.

pharmacy

KNOW YOUR FOODSTUFF There is no denying that flavour and avoiding chemicals are beneficial, but it is equally important to understand the nutritional advantages of eating organic food. Crops grown organically, harvested at the peak of their natural condition and consumed within days supply a fuller range of nutrients. Not only do you get everything that nature intended from organic produce, you get it in greater abundance. There is growing evidence of the nutritional superiority of organic food over crops grown in denatured soil and animals fed on synthetic feeds and prematurely matured by growth promoters, antibiotics and hormones. In the following pages you will learn exactly what you are eating and why. And this is something that we can all gain from.

food	source of	organic
Alfalfa sprouts	Vitamin A and C, B vitamins E and K, calcium, silicon	Grown under natural conditions, sprouts contain all the essential nutrients necessary to produce an entire healthy plant.
Apples	Carotenes, pectin, vitamin C, potassium, ellagic acid	Allowed to ripen on the tree and picked at maturity, organic apples have a much higher vitamin content. Orchards grazed by livestock will be naturally fertilised, yielding a richer mineral content in the fruit.
Apricots	Beta-carotene, potassium, iron, soluble fibre	Richer in beta-carotene, vitamin C and essential minerals than non-organic counterparts. Dried organic apricots a re more nutritious and are not subjected to mineral oil treatment.
Artichokes (Jerusalem and globe)	Inulin, phosphorus, iron	Organic Jerusalem and globe artichokes are allowed to reach the peak of their therapeutic and nutritional value.
Asparagus	Vitamin C, riboflavin, folic acid, asparagine, potassium, phosphorus	Organic asparagus boasts superior flavour. It is only available during the appropriate but short season, but will provide maximum nutritional benefits.
Avocado	Potassium, vitamins E and A, essential fatty acids	Since they're not picked at an under-ripe stage and artificially ripened, they possess the full range of essential fatty acids which only develops during the natural ripening process.
Bananas	Potassium, fibre, energy, magnesium, vitamin A, folic acid	Only organically grown bananas are free of residues. For this reason, it is vital to choose only organic bananas for use in baby foods.
Basil	Volatile oils: linalol, limonene, estragole	Organic basil is grown in humus-rich soil, and therefore develops a full quota of volatile oils.
Beans, dried	Protein, carbohydrates, fibre, B vitamins, minerals, folic acid, selenium, iron, zinc. Choose chickpeas for calcium, soy beans for cancer- and osteoporosis-fighting genistein	Choosing only organic beans is essential if you want to avoid dangerous chemicals. This is especially relevant for vegetarians, who rely on these legumes as their staple source of protein.

good for	non-organic
The nervous system, bones and skin.	Sprouts grown using an industrial water supply may contain excessive nitrites and nitrates. May sometimes be treated with fungicides.
The immune system, digestion, heart and circulation. Especially good for constipation, diarrhoea and lowering of cholesterol.	Sprayed many times while growing, specifically with fungicides, insecticides, herbicides and growth regulators to speed up or slow down maturation levels. Organophosphates widely used. After harvest, usually treated with wax, which often contains preservatives.
Skin and respiratory problems; protects against cancer. Dried apricots relieve constipation and high blood pressure.	Most apricots are imported, and therefore liable to be heavily treated during growth. Fungicides, herbicides and insecticides are among the most common sprays. Multiple residues are found in a high proportion of non-organic fruits such as apricots, hence they should never be puréed as baby food.
Digestion, as they stimulate liver and gall-bladder function. Useful for gout, arthritis and rheumatism.	Globe artichoke are likely to be more heavily sprayed with herbicides and fungicides. Parathion, phthalate and alkyl aryl polyethylene glycols are widely used on US crops.
Gentle diuretic treatment, hence it is excellent for cystitis and fluid retention. Good for rheumatism and arthritis, but not for gout.	Commercial crops are heavily treated, particularly with methyl bromide, paraquat and synthetic pyrethrums.
Heart, circulation and skin. Relieves symptoms of PMS, and protects against cancer.	The organophosphate insecticide malathion is widely used on non-organic avocados, together with methyl bromide, and other persistent pesticides.
Preventing cramp. Excellent for digestion, chronic fatigue syndrome and glandular fever.	Although most are present in the skins, residues have been found in almost every non-organic banana sample. Fungicide residues are common, as well as a mixture of pesticides.
Stimulating the digestion and as a calming, stress-fighting herb.	Sometimes grown hydroponically, non-organic herbs can have poor nutrient and essential oil levels. Likely to be sprayed with insecticides and fungicides.
Maintaining a healthy heart and circulatory system, also fighting high blood pressure and lowering cholesterol. Offers excellent protection against cancer and regulates bowel function.	Many non-organic beans are imported from countries where control of agrochemicals may not be as strict as it should be. Some of the most toxic of agrochemicals – including the highly toxic herbicide aldicarb, the fungicide captan, lindane, methyl bromide and paraquat – are used heavily on all bean crops.

food	source of	organic
Beans, green	Vitamins A and C, potassium, folic acid	Organic varieties naturally taste better. Fresh organic beans are also ideal puréed as an early baby food (for babies of four to five months onwards).
Beetroot	Vitamins B_6 and C, beta-carotene, potassium, folic acid, iron, calcium	Organic ones are best for deep colour and flavour, and absorb more vital minerals and nutrients from richer, balanced soil.
Blackberries	Vitamins E and C, potassium, fibre, cancer-fighting phytochemicals	Hand-picked wild blackberries have the best flavour and tend to be more nutritious than cultivated varieties. Commercial organic berries have more vitamin E and minerals than non-organic counterparts.
Blackcurrants	Vitamin C, carotenoids, anti-inflammatory and cancer-fighting phytochemicals	Organic blackcurrants are essential for use in juices designed for children as well as for jam making. Their natural flavour and acidity are much more pronounced than non-organic examples.
Blueberries	Vitamin C, carotenoids, antibacterial and cancer-fighting phytochemicals	Organically grown blueberries have a better flavour, and they are richer in natural plant chemicals, especially antibacterial substances.
Brazil nuts	Protein, selenium, vitamin E, B vitamins	Choosing organic is the only way to guarantee chemical-free nuts.
Bread	Fibre, iron, B vitamins, vitamin E, protein	Organic bread is more delicious, with huge health benefits. Whether wholemeal or unbleached stone-ground white, it's far richer in nutrients than non-organic loaves. Note: bread made with organic flour is not necessarily organic; it may contain a range of additives. Check that each loaf is certified organic, or that the baker displays a registered logo.
Broccoli	Vitamins A and C, folic acid, riboflavin, potassium, iron, cancer-fighting phytochemicals	Organically grown broccoli boasts a richer mineral content, especially of iron and sulphur, because of better soil quality.

good for	non-organic
Skin, hair and digestive problems.	In the UK, non-organic beans are rather less sprayed than many other crops, yet they are still usually treated with herbicides and insecticides. In the US, however, green beans are treated the same as dried beans (*see* page 24).
Anaemia, chronic fatigue and convalescence.	Non-organic beets are treated with fungicides, herbicides and insecticides, (dichloropropene and malathion); also sometimes lindane. In storage, they are often treated with fungicides – including systemic ones.
Heart, circulation and skin. Also good protection against cancer.	Commercial blackberries are heavily sprayed with multiple herbicides, insecticides and especially fungicides; metalaxyl, malathion, paraquat and the organophosphate chlorpyrifos are commonly used.
The immune system. Also protect against colds, 'flu and some cancers. Good for lowering blood pressure and reducing stress.	*See* Blackberries.
See Blackberries.	*See* Blackberries.
One of the richest sources of selenium (five provide a day's dose), an essential mineral that protects against heart disease, breast and prostate cancer.	Like most nuts, non-organic Brazils will contain systemic insecticides in their kernels. Pesticides and fungicides are widely used in standard commercial harvesting.
Everyone – except those with wheat intolerance. Especially valuable for combating stress, physically active people, and the prevention of constipation, diverticulitis and piles.	As well as the many multiple applications of chemicals applied to growing wheat, organophosphates and methyl bromide are widely used on the crop after harvesting. In addition, conditioners, flour improvers, flour extenders, preservatives and flavourings are added to non-organic bread.
Anaemia, chronic fatigue, before and during pregnancy, skin problems and protection against cancer.	*See* Cabbage family.

food	source of	organic
Brussels sprouts	Especially rich in cancer-fighting phytochemicals, vitamin C and beta-carotene	Slower maturation times mean higher concentrations of phytochemicals and more soil-derived nutrients in organic crops.
Cabbage family (brassicas)	Vitamins A, C, E, folic acid, potassium, cancer-fighting phytochemicals	Because they are grown in richer soil, organic cabbages have a higher food value than non-organic specimens.
Carrots	Vitamin A, carotenoids, folic acid, potassium, magnesium	The high concentration of nutrients in the skin of organic carrots provides better food value and value for money, since there is no need to peel them before eating.
Cauliflower	Vitamin C, folic acid, sulphur	*See* Cabbage family.
Celeriac	Vitamin C, folic acid, potassium, fibre	*See* Carrots.
Celery	Beta-carotene, potassium, vitamin C, coumarins, flavonoids, fibre	The stems and leaves are rich in beta-carotenes, and in organic celery, these are safe to eat.
Chard (Swiss)	Vitamins A and C, iron, calcium, phosphorus, carotenes, cancer-fighting phytochemicals	Chard is a "cut and come again" crop – which makes it even more important to choose organic examples as otherwise the same root will concentrate all chemical applications.
Cheese	Protein, calcium and vitamin B_{12}. Also a valuable source of zinc, essential for normal growth, reproduction (especially sperm production) and immunity	Nearly all organic cheeses are made by small traditional cheesemakers, so the quality and flavour of the product are superb. The nutritional value of organically produced unpasteurised milk is inevitably higher, so organic cheeses have higher calcium and protein values.
Cherries	Vitamin C, potassium, magnesium, flavonoids, cancer-fighting phytochemicals	Fruits are free from all chemical residues.

good for	non-organic
Protection against cancer, skin problems.	*See* Cabbage family.
Protection against cancer, stomach ulcers, chest infections, skin problems, anaemia.	All brassicas are heavily sprayed with insecticides, herbicides and fungicides, including organophosphates which affect nerves and muscles in large doses; methyl bromide; lindane; paraquat; anti-slug treatments such as metaldehyde. For this reason, never use the outer leaves of non-organic brassicas.
Eyesight, circulation, and protection against heart disease and cancer. Also good for the skin and all mucous membranes.	Commercially grown carrots are heavily sprayed with multiple applications of insecticides, herbicides and fungicides, including organophosphates, anti-slug treatments, methyl bromide and paraquat. Commercial seeds are also usually pre-treated. Non-organic carrots accumulate nitrates from artificial fertilisers, so they must be peeled, topped and tailed before consumption.
Protection against cancer, natural immunity and skin problems.	*See* Cabbage family.
Pre-pregnancy and pregnancy, constipation and lowering cholesterol levels.	*See* Carrots.
Fluid retention, constipation, rheumatism, gout, arthritis and stress.	*See* Carrots.
Protection against eye diseases such as macular degeneration. Also protection against cancer and good for anaemia.	Fungicides, herbicides and insecticides are likely to be used on non-organic chard, in addition to slug deterrents.
Bones, teeth, and prevention/treatment of osteoporosis. Excellent pre-conceptual, pregnancy and breastfeeding food (avoid unpasteurised ones).	The main concern about non-organic cheeses is the accumulation of antibiotics which come into milk via the food chain. This regular low-level intake almost certainly causes the development of resistant strains of bacteria. In addition, many persistent organochloride pesticides – specifically lindane – accumulate in fat, and find their way into dairy products.
Natural resistance, arthritis and rheumatism, protection against cancer. Especially good for gout.	Many British growers do not spray their cherry orchards, but those that do use herbicides, fungicides and insecticides. Imported crops are nearly always treated with a wide range of toxic chemicals.

food	source of	organic
Chestnuts	Fibre, vitamins E and B$_6$, potassium	Organically grown chestnuts are free from toxic chemicals.
Chicory	Folic acid, potassium, iron, vitamins C and A (the latter only if unblanched), liver-stimulating terpenoids	Whether the tight-bunched variety or curly endive, the outer darker leaves of chicory contain the most valuable nutritional components. These can be eaten safely only if they have been grown organically.
Chillies	Vitamin C, carotenoids, capsaicin	Biological pest control is used by organic growers for all members of the pepper family. Professional chefs maintain that organic chillies are the hottest.
Coriander	Flavonoids, coumarins, linalol	Grown in properly fertilised, naturally balanced soil, organic coriander is richer in nutrients and active components.
Courgettes and other curcubits	Beta-carotenes, vitamin C, folic acid, potassium	Organic examples are best for flavour and nutrient density.
Cranberries	Vitamin C, cancer-fighting phytochemicals, specific urinary antibacterials	Organically grown cranberries will contain a higher content of valuable nutrients.
Cucumber	Tiny amounts of beta-carotene in the skin, also a little silica, potassium, and folic acid	*See* Courgettes and other curcubits.
Dandelion leaves	Beta-carotene, other carotenoids, iron, diuretic, liver-stimulating phytochemicals	Organically managed dandelion plants are free from chemical sprays. If grown in your own garden or allotment, they're also free of charge.
Dates	Iron, potassium, folic acid, fibre, fruit sugar	Fresh or naturally dried fruits will contain greater concentrations of nutrients without risk of chemical residues.

good for	non-organic
Energy. They are also easily digestible and make excellent gluten-free flour for those with wheat allergies.	Virtually all chestnuts in the UK are imported, so it is difficult to know what prior treatments they may have had. Highly likely to have been treated with methyl bromide.
Before and during pregnancy. Has excellent detoxifying and cleansing properties, and is mildly diuretic and liver stimulating.	Like all salad crops, non-organic chicory is subject to multiple sprayings of insecticides, herbicides and especially fungicides, if grown under glass or in poly-tunnels. Slug deterrents are on the increase. Phthalates, oxyethylenes, and herbicides are heavily used in other countries, especially the US.
Circulation, especially helpful for chilblains; sinus, digestion, chest problems. Fights stomach bugs.	Virtually all imported chillies are sprayed with insecticides and herbicides and treated with fungicides.
Digestion. Relieves wind, bloating, irritable bowel syndrome, stress.	Non-organic examples may be treated with phthalates. Like other herbs, they may be grown hydroponically, and may be deficient in some nutrients.
Skin problems, natural resistance and weight loss.	Courgettes, cucumbers, marrows, pumpkins and squashes are not generally very heavily treated with chemicals. Most commonly used are fungicides and herbicides. Imported crops may be subject to more severe chemical treatments, including paraquat, synthetic pyrethrins and various herbicides.
Treatment/prevention of cystitis. Powerful cancer-fighter and immune system booster.	Because they're grown in bogs, the purity of cranberries is only as good as the water that surrounds them. If it is polluted, the fruit is likely to absorb toxic chemicals. Non-organic fruit is often sprayed with fungicides after harvest.
Skin and eyes. The juice is useful for relieving fevers.	Usually waxed. See Courgettes and other curcubits.
Fluid retention, bloating, liver problems, PMS.	When available commercially, they're imported and likely to be treated like other commercial salad crops. See Chicory.
Anaemia, fatigue, constipation, pregnancy. An excellent and easily digested energy source before and during sport.	Non-organic examples are subject to after-harvest treatments with oils and fungicides.

food	source of	organic
Eggs	Protein, vitamin B_{12}, iron, lecithin. Also a good source of zinc and vitamins A, D and E	All organic eggs are also free range, but free range does not necessarily mean organic, as the hens may be ranging on pastures that have been chemically treated. Only organic eggs are free from all traces of antibiotics and chemical food additives.
Fennel	Low in vitamins, but rich in volatile oils, including fenchone, anethole and anisic acid – all liver and digestive stimulants	Organic plants contain a greater concentration of active ingredients.
Figs	Beta-carotene, iron, potassium, fibre ficin (a digestive aid), cancer-fighting phytochemicals	Fresh or dried, organic figs will have a richer, fuller flavour and higher concentration of nutrients, especially ficin.
Fish	Protein, B vitamins, minerals – especially iron, zinc and iodine. Oily fish has the added bonus of vitamin D and essential fatty acids	Organically farmed fish are beginning to appear on the market.
Garlic	Antibacterial and anti-fungal sulphur compounds, cancer-fighting and heart-protective phytochemicals	Organic examples will contain higher concentrations of the sulphur compound, allicin.
Ginger	Circulatory-stimulating zingiberene and gingerol	Like all the aromatic spices, organically grown examples will have a fuller, stronger flavour due to a better quality plant.
Grapes	Vitamin C, natural sugars, powerful antioxidant flavonoids	Organically grown grapes have a higher sugar content due to natural ripening, and are richer in anthocyanins and flavones.

good for	non-organic
Protection against cancer and heart disease; cholesterol stories are untrue. Also helps relieve anaemia, rheumatoid arthritis, osteoarthritis and supports the male sexual function.	Non-organic eggs contain chemicals derived from non-organic feed; also antibiotics, hormones, and any other chemicals fed or injected into the bird.
Digestive problems, flatulence, and fluid retention.	Herbicides and fungicides are most commonly used on non-organic examples, together with synthetic pyrethrins and, in the US, dicloran.
Energy, constipation, digestive problems, anaemia and protection against cancer.	Fresh figs are heavily treated with malathion, methyl bromide and paraquat. Dried ones are treated with fungicides and oils.
Oily fish: joint diseases, brain development, pregnancy, and all inflammatory diseases. *White fish:* heart protection. *Shellfish:* male sexual function, heart protection.	Traces of pesticide have been found in most varieties of fish, in spite of which fish is still an excellent food source. Farmed salmon and trout may, but rarely do, contain antibiotic residues, but organophosphates have not been detected.
Preventing heart disease, lowering cholesterol levels, high blood pressure. Useful as an anti-fungal and antibacterial agent, and helps relieve sinus and chest infections.	Like its relatives, onions, spring onions and leeks, garlic is most heavily treated with herbicides and fungicides; insecticides are used only occasionally. Synthetic pyrethrums and organophosphates such as clorpyrifos and triazophos are commonly used, and imported crops are likely to be treated with malathion, methomyl and fenamiphos.
Morning sickness in pregnancy, travel sickness, post-operative sickness, circulation, fevers and coughs.	Imported examples are heavily treated with methyl bromide and fungicides.
Convalescence, anaemia, fatigue, cancer protection and weight gain, especially after illness.	Commercially produced grapes are heavily treated with a wide range of insecticides, herbicides and fungicides. Copper sulphates, chlorpyrifos, phenamyfos, malathion, and heavy use of methyl bromide, together with paraquat, are just a few of the chemicals.

food	source of	organic
Grapefruit	Vitamin C, beta-carotene, potassium, bioflavonoids – especially naringin, which thins the blood and lowers cholesterol	Choosing organic grapefruit is especially important if you're using the skin. They will also contain higher concentrations of naringin and more vitamin C.
Kale	Beta-carotene, vitamin C, phosphorus, sulphur, iron, potassium, calcium, folic acid, cancer-fighting phytochemicals	Flavour is the key factor, and organic kale is instantly distinguishable from its pale commercial counterpart.
Kiwi fruit	Vitamin C, beta-carotene, potassium, bioflavonoids, fibre	Although richer in acidic vitamin C, organic kiwi fruits have a much fuller and sweeter flavour.
Kohlrabi	Vitamin C, folic acid, potassium, cancer-fighting phytochemicals	Sometimes called the "turnip cabbage", both the root ball and leaves are eaten; therefore it is especially important to choose chemical free organic examples.
Lamb's lettuce	Vitamins A, C and B$_6$, folic acid, iron, potassium, zinc. Contains calming phytochemicals	To produce its valuable phytochemicals, this plant needs rich, balanced soil which only organic growing can provide.
Leeks	Vitamins A and C, folic acid, potassium, diuretic, anti-arthritic, anti-inflammatory, cancer-fighting phytochemicals	This valuable member of the allium family spends its growing life buried in the soil from which it derives its great therapeutic value. For optimum benefits, organic growing is a must.
Lemons	Vitamin C, bioflavonoids, potassium, limonene	One of the most valuable members of the citrus-fruit family, the lemon is much more than something to put in your G&T. Its vitamin C and bioflavonoid content is markedly higher in organic versions.
Lettuce	Vitamins A and C, folic acid, potassium, calcium, phosphorus, sleep-inducing phytochemicals	There are many varieties of lettuce, but in all organically produced plants, the outer leaves are darker and contain more valuable carotenoids. Because you can eat this without risk, the overall nutritional value is higher.

good for	non-organic
Natural resistance, circulatory problems, sore throats and bleeding gums.	Non-organic citrus-fruit orchards are subjected to multiple heavy applications of a wide variety of potentially toxic chemicals. The US Department of Pesticide Regulation lists more than 100 substances, including oxyethylenes, polyethylenes, carbaryl, copper sulphate, diazinon, methyl bromide, paraquat and pyrethrins which may be used on citrus fruits. After-harvest treatments with waxes and anti-fungals are routine.
Protection against cancer; provides a boost to immunity. Good for skin and eyes thanks to high content of beta-carotene.	*See* Cabbage family.
The immune system, skin, constipation and digestive problems.	Non-organic crops are regularly sprayed with a wide range of pesticides, some of which are systemic and therefore not removed with the peel.
Protection against cancer, resistance, and skin problems.	*See* Cabbage family.
Anaemia, stress and anxiety. Great before/during pregnancy, and when breastfeeding.	*See* Chicory.
Chest and voice problems, especially sore throats. Helps reduce high blood pressure and cholesterol, and is particularly good for gout and arthritis.	*See* Garlic.
This powerful immune booster is also good for digestive problems. Particularly beneficial for mouth ulcers and gum disease.	*See* Grapefruit.
Insomnia, stress and bronchitis.	Lettuce in particular tends to concentrate nitrates from synthetic fertiliser. *See also* Chicory.

food	source of	organic
Lime	Vitamin C, bioflavonoids, potassium, limonene	Organic limes have a higher vitamin C content, more bioflavonoids and a wonderful flavour.
Mango	Vitamin C, beta-carotene, potassium, flavonoids, other antioxidants	As with all tropical fruits, naturally grown mangoes which are picked as near to ripeness as possible achieve maximum nutritional value, sugar content and sweetness.
Meat	Protein, iron, B vitamins, other minerals	By choosing organically reared meat, you know the animal has been reared and kept under welfare-friendly conditions. Organic butchers take pride, time and trouble in correct storage, hanging and preparation, so your produce arrives in peak condition and perfectly prepared. It's worth reducing your overall meat consumption (it's healthier anyway) to pay the extra cost – not just in terms of wonderful flavour but peace of mind as well. Don't forget that free range doesn't mean organic, but organic always means free range.
Melon	Vitamins A, C; potassium, folic acid, some B vitamins	Melons use gallons of water as they grow. Low nutrient levels are even further reduced unless grown in quality organic soil.
Milk	Calcium, riboflavin, zinc, protein	Though maligned by many alternative practitioners, organic milk is an excellent source of valuable nutrients for most people. Organic is essential to avoid chemical contamination, particularly where small children are concerned.
Mint	Antispasmodic volatile oils, menthol, flavonoids	As with all aromatic herbs, the final content of volatile oils (which provide medicinal benefits) is entirely dependent on the quality of soil in which the plants are growing. Only organic soil can provide optimum conditions.
Mushrooms	Some protein, vitamins B_{12} and E, zinc	Wild or field mushrooms from organic sources are the most delicious and nutritious available. Organic cultivated mushrooms are superior to their commercial rivals.
Nuts and seeds	Protein, unsaturated fats, minerals (especially zinc and selenium), fibre, energy	It is important to consume organic versions of nuts and seeds wherever possible, as many systemic chemicals are concentrated in these two food groups.

good for	non-organic
Resistance, and terrific for the relief of coughs colds and 'flu. Also highly cancer-fighting.	*See* Grapefruit.
Convalescence, skin problems, protection against cancer and a boost to the immune system.	Post-harvest treatment with fungicides is most common, but some synthetic pyrethrums and other insecticides are used.
Anaemia, stress, and all-round nutrition, as meat contains a broad spread of essential nutrients.	Organochloride pesticides tend to be accumulated and stored in animal fat. Imported meat is particularly suspect; high residues, for example, have been found in New Zealand lamb and Chinese rabbit. The current controversy over growth hormones in US beef has so far prohibited its importation into Europe, as the amount of chemicals used on animal fodder crops in the States is horrendous. Captan, carbaryl, diquat, paraquat, parathion, methyl bromide and a hundred other potentially harmful substances are used with scant regard for the consequences. Antibiotics are another major concern in non-organic meat; they're often fed automatically as growth promoters and used illegally and indiscriminately for the treatment of illness in non-organic animal husbandry.
Mild constipation, gout, arthritis and urinary problems.	Some really unpleasant chemicals are used on melons, including large amounts of methyl bromide, lindane, paraquat and synthetic pyrethrums.
Growth, strong bones and convalescence.	*See* Cheese.
Indigestion, irritable bowel syndrome, gastritis, bloating and flatulence.	*See* Coriander.
Important nutrient for vegetarians and vegans. Valuable for depression, anxiety and fatigue.	As well as fungicides and pesticides used on the crops themselves, large amounts are required for the sterilisation of the growing medium and sheds in non-organic varieties.
Diabetes male sexual function, fertility, constipation and varicose veins. Also cancer-fighting.	Non-organic nuts and seeds contain systemic insecticides, and nearly all are treated with fungicides. All are commonly exposed to methyl bromide.

food	source of	organic
Oats	Calcium, potassium, magnesium, B-complex vitamins, some vitamin E	Like all cereals, the nutritional value of oats is dependent on the soil quality in which they grow. Organic versions are better nutritionally, and are particularly important for babies and children because they are free of chemicals.
Olives	Protective antioxidants, vitamin E and mono-unsaturated oil	Organic olives are chemical free while growing and during processing. They boast more vitamin E and superior flavour.
Onions	Vitamin C, sulphur-based phytochemicals similar to garlic	The higher content of the enzyme allinase releases an equally higher content of sulphurous compounds; these not only make you cry but give organic onions more flavour.
Oranges (mandarins, satsumas, tangerines)	Vitamins C and B_6, bioflavonoids, potassium, limonene, thiamine, folic acid, calcium, iron	For optimum vitamin C levels, oranges need to be grown organically.
Pak choi	Vitamin C, beta-carotene, folic acid, B vitamins, cancer-fighting phytochemicals	This most famous of the oriental brassicas only develops its full nutritional potential when grown organically.
Parsley	Vitamins A and C, iron, calcium, potassium	Parsley's rich mineral content depends entirely on the nutrients available in the soil. Only organic growing provides all the essentials.
Parsnip	Vitamin E, folic acid, potassium, B vitamins, inulin	This delicious but much maligned root vegetable grows deep into the soil and depends on deep, rich, organic beds for perfect growth, flavour and nutritional value.
Pawpaw	Vitamin C, beta-carotene, flavonoids, magnesium, the digestive enzyme papain	Like other tropical fruits, pawpaws are at their nutritional best when harvested as close to ripeness as possible – as when organically grown and shipped for immediate consumption.
Peaches	Beta-carotene, flavonoids, vitamin C, potassium	Organic peaches have a flavour and texture of a totally different dimension, and contain significantly higher proportions of valuable nutrients.

good for	non-organic
Reducing blood cholesterol, stress, digestion. Specifically protective against bowel cancer, heart disease and high blood pressure.	*See* Wheat.
Skin, heart and circulation.	Multiple applications of a variety of pesticides are used on olives in some parts of the world.
Reducing cholesterol, preventing blood clots, bronchitis, asthma, chest infections, gout, arthritis and chilblains.	*See* Garlic.
Fighting infection and improving resistance, fighting heart disease and high blood pressure.	*See* Grapefruit.
Cancer protection, boosting immunity, anaemia, pregnancy and skin problems.	*See* Cabbage family.
A strong diuretic and anti-inflammatory, parsley is good for relieving fluid retention, PMS, gout, rheumatoid and osteoarthritis. Also useful against anaemia.	*See* Coriander.
Fatigue, constipation, pregnancy and diabetes.	*See* Carrots.
Digestive problems, skin, improved immunity. Also for convalescence, particularly after gastric illness as they are extremely easy to digest.	Post-harvest treatment with fungicides is most common, but some synthetic pyrethrums and other insecticides are used.
Pregnancy, people on low-salt diets, reducing cholesterol. Also good as a gentle laxative.	Non-organic crops are treated extensively with insecticides, pesticides, herbicides and fungicides. Captan, chlorpyrifos, diazinon, malathion, parathion, methyl bromide and paraquat are heavily used in the US.

food	source of	organic
Pears	Soluble fibre, vitamin C	Pear-skin contains a large proportion of nutrients, particularly fibre. Only organic ones are absolutely safe to eat unpeeled.
Peas	Thiamine (B_1), folic acid, beta-carotene, vitamin C, protein	Nutritional quality and flavour are entirely dependent on soil quality, which is why organic peas are sweeter and healthier.
Peppers	Vitamin C, beta-carotene, folic acid, potassium; phytochemicals that prevent blood clots, strokes and heart disease	Organic peppers are grown in soil, not water, so they develop a better texture, better flavour and a higher nutritional content.
Pineapple	Vitamin C, but most valuable for enzymes, especially bromelain	Once picked, pineapples don't ripen, they rot. Thus, they are ideally harvested at perfection for immediate consumption – the standard practice of organic pineapple farmers.
Plums	Beta-carotene, vitamins C and E, malic acid	Buying organic plums means that there are no worries about eating the skin, which is a good source of fibre.
Potatoes	Rich in vitamin C, fibre, B vitamins; contain some minerals	Organic potatoes are immediately distinguishable by their superb flavour.
Poultry	Protein, vitamin B_{12}, iron, zinc	Not only does organic poultry taste infinitely superior, it is your only guarantee that the meat contains no unwanted chemicals. Note: free range does not mean organic, but organic always means free range.
Prunes	Beta-carotene, niacin, vitamin B_6, potassium, iron, fibre, phytochemicals	Made from organically grown plums and naturally dried, they have much more intense flavour and no added chemicals.
Pumpkin	Vitamins A, C; potassium, folic acid; some B vitamins	Organic pumpkins are allowed to grow more slowly, and thus develop a deeper colour, fuller flavour and more nutrients.

good for	non-organic
Energy, lowering cholesterol, convalescence and constipation.	Residues of non-approved chemicals are frequently found on domestic and imported pears. Multiple applications of long-acting sprays are common.
Protein, stress, tension and all digestive problems.	Herbicides are used heavily on peas. Imported crops are likely to be sprayed with captan, paraquat and parathion.
All skin problems, mucous membranes, night and colour vision. Also a good booster for the immune system.	Non-organic peppers may look perfect, but they are frequently grown hydroponically, which results in reduced flavour, texture and nutrient quality. Organophosphates and synthetic pyrethrums are widely used on non-organic crops, while methyl bromide is used heavily in the US.
Angina, arthritis, constipation, fevers, sore throats and all soft tissue injuries.	Insecticides, herbicides and fungicides are used heavily during production, followed by fumigants and more fungicides after harvest.
Heart, circulation, fluid retention, and digestion.	Non-organic plums are subjected to rounds of insecticides, fungicides and herbicides. Imported varieties are more likely to have been heavily treated.
Anaemia, digestive problems, fatigue, growth and natural resistance.	Non-organic potatoes are treated heavily throughout growth with repeated applications of insecticides, herbicides and fungicides. Seed potatoes may also be treated. Potatoes in store are treated with fungicides and growth regulators. Organophosphates and long-acting herbicides such as paraquat are widely used. Imported varieties are often exposed to even greater doses.
Convalescence, anaemia, natural resistance, PMS, pregnancy and growth.	As well as all the chemical residues in the non-organic feed on which they're reared, non-organic chickens may well have been given prophylactic medication in their food, including antibiotics.
High blood pressure, fatigue, exhaustion and constipation. Also contain high concentrations of cancer-fighting phytochemicals.	*See* Plums. After drying, non-organic prunes are treated with oils and fungicides.
Protection against cancer, respiratory problems and skin disorders.	*See* Courgettes.

food	source of	organic
Radishes	Vitamin C, iron, magnesium, sulphur, potassium, phytochemicals	As the radish develops in the soil, there is a greater chance of absorption of chemicals, especially from the skin which is rich in nutrients. Hence, organic versions are a must.
Raspberries	Vitamin C, soluble fibre; calcium, potassium, iron, magnesium	Since raspberries retain the most flavour if they are unwashed, it is essential to choose organic ones.
Rhubarb	Calcium, potassium, manganese; some vitamin A and C	Organic rhubarb has a delicate and delicious flavour.
Rice, brown	Protein, B vitamins	Choose organic versions to avoid accumulations of toxic chemicals stored in the liver and body fat.
Spinach	Chlorophyll, folic acid, beta-carotene, lutein, xeaxanthine, iron, cancer-fighting phytochemicals	Organically grown varieties have a higher chlorophyll and folic acid content, and are generally slightly less bitter.
Spring greens	Vitamin C, beta-carotene, carotenoids, iron, cancer-fighting phytochemicals	Organic versions contain considerably higher concentrations of phytochemicals.
Strawberries	Vitamins C and E, beta-carotene, anti-arthritic phytochemicals, soluble fibre	Organic versions show superb flavour and texture compared with commercial varieties.
Swede	Vitamin C, useful amounts of vitamin A, trace minerals	Swedes are in close contact with soil contaminants, so buying organic ensures that none are present. Their mineral content is entirely dependent on soil quality.
Sweetcorn	Fibre, protein, some vitamins A and E; some B vitamins, folic acid	Organic examples are naturally ripened, which results in a higher sugar content and improved flavour.

good for	non-organic
Protection against cancer, liver and gall bladder problems, indigestion and respiratory problems.	Non-organic radishes are treated regularly with insecticides, herbicides, fungicides and molluscicides, including systemic chemicals and organophosphates, particularly chlorpyrifos.
Immune system, protection against cancer and mouth ulcers.	Non-organic raspberries are heavily sprayed with fungicides, herbicides, insecticides and slug deterrents. Synthetic pyrethrums are widely used.
Relieving constipation.	Non-organic rhubarb is often grown in poor soil and is often forced, so it will have a lower in nutrient content. Pyrethrums are most commonly used.
People with coeliac disease as it contains no gluten; diarrhoea. Excellent source of energy.	There is very little control over pesticides in some countries in which it is grown. Residues of methyl bromide are frequently found, but many other chemicals are regularly used. Toxic residues are more common in brown rice.
Skin, protection against cancer, prevention of vision loss in old age. Also good before and during pregnancy.	Grown by lettuce growers, especially baby spinach leaves for salads, so will be treated in similar fashion; *see* Chicory. Also frequently contains high levels of nitrates – often exceeding EU recommended limits – which can be hazardous to babies and very small children.
Protection against cancer, skin problems and anaemia.	*See* Cabbage.
Protection against cancer, gout, arthritis, kidney problems and anaemia.	Non-organic crops are sprayed heavily with multiple applications of fungicides, herbicides, insecticides and slug deterrents, particularly organochlorides and organophosphates. Lindane, captan, methyl bromide, paraquat and parathion are all commonly used on imported crops.
Protection against cancer, skin problems, and an ideal weaning food for babies.	*See* Parsnip.
Energy and fibre.	Most non-organic examples are sprayed with herbicides, but organophosphate pesticides are also widely used.

food	source of	organic
Sweet potato	Vitamins C and E, beta-carotene and other carotenoids, protein, cancer-fighting phytochemicals	Choose organic when buying root vegetables such as sweet potatoes not only for better flavour and nutrition, but to ensure the absence of chemical residues.
Tea	Vitamins E and K, protective phenolic compounds. Also trace minerals, tannin, and powerful protective antioxidants	Organic benefits are as much for the growers as for the consumer. Organic teas have a wonderful flavour and contain no chemical residues – which means that those who pick them are not at risk from the chemicals, either.
Tofu and other soy products	Protein and enormous quantities of cancer-fighting genisteine	Buying organic soya products is your only guarantee that they will be free of genetic modification.
Tomatoes	Vitamins C and E, potassium, beta-carotene, lycopene	The more interesting varieties are usually organically grown and offer much better flavour, smell and nutritional quality.
Watercress	Vitamins C and E, beta-carotene, antibacterial mustard oils, phenethyl isothiocyanate, iron	Organically produced watercress is bursting with flavour and that wonderful mustardy, peppery bite no longer present in non-organic varieties.
Wheat, wholegrain	B-complex vitamins, vitamin E, fibre, zinc, magnesium and (if North American or Canadian) selenium	Organic wheat is grown in rich, naturally composted soil to achieve maximum nutritional value and protein content at point of harvest.
Wine	Excellent source of heart-protective substances	It's not enough that the grapes are grown organically; check that the wine itself is certified organic, as many chemicals are added during the winemaking process.
Yoghurt	Calcium, riboflavin, zinc, protein, beneficial ba cteria	Organic yoghurt is the only guarantee of a high-quality nutritional product that is free from antibiotic or other chemical residues.

good for	non-organic
Eye problems, night vision and all skin problems. Also a powerful cancer-fighting food.	Like ordinary potatoes, non-organic sweet potatoes are subject to multiple applications of herbicides and pesticides. Chlorpyrifos, malathion, methyl bromide, methomyl and metalaxyl are among the most common.
Mild stimulant for fatigue and exhaustion. Also cancer-fighting and heart protective.	Non-organic tea is subjected to a very intensive round of pesticides, especially paraquat, which is a major health risk for plantation workers. Little residue, however, remains in the finished product.
Protection against cancer – especially breast and prostate. Good for vegetarians, diabetics. Good replacement for those with milk intolerance.	All soya products originate from soya beans, which are treated with organophosphates, herbicides and other pesticides. In the US, it is almost impossible to separate GM beans from non-GM ones, making non-organic soya products doubly hazardous.
Protection against cancer, skin problems, fertility and heart protection.	Chemical residues have been found in more than half the UK-produced tomatoes and in 60 per cent of imported crops. Non-organic versions are often grown hydroponically. Fungicides, methyl bromide, mevinphos, paraquat, parathion, and many other chemicals are used on crops grown outside the UK.
Essential protection against lung cancer. Food poisoning, anaemia, skin and underactive thyroid.	Non-organic examples run the double hazard of pollutants in the water – especially nitrate runoff from synthetic fertilisers – and treatment with insecticides and slug deterrents.
A vital source of energy and essential nutrients.	Non-organic cereal grains are often grown in "dust bowl" areas by intensive monocropping of vast acreages. Massive amounts of synthetic fertilisers are applied, as well as herbicides, insecticides and fungicides, including persistent organophosphates and synthetic pyrethrums. Lindane, paraquat and methyl bromide are common.
The heart (in modest doses) improves circulation and helps mild depression.	Grape-growing is an intensive agribusiness. It takes up only a small percentage of land, but those acres are treated with hugely disproportionate amounts of insecticides and herbicides.
Diarrhoea, natural resistance, prevention and treatment of osteoporosis, thrush and cystitis.	*See* Cheese.

or

cooking
ganic

preparation
of organic food

Having gone to all the extra trouble and expense of buying organic food, don't waste the additional bonus of organic nutrients by not taking proper care of produce when you get it home.

Keep it in the dark

I'm always horrified at the way many people put the vegetable rack in that little gap between the cooker and the dishwasher, or leave their fruit looking wonderfully decorative in front of a sunlit window. As soon as a fruit or vegetable is harvested, it begins to lose some of its nutrient value; for optimum benefit, then, store produce in cool, dark conditions and consume as soon as possible. Generally speaking, root vegetables and hard fruits such as apples and pears lose their nutrients very slowly. However, soft fruits, tropical fruits, green leafy vegetables and salad items can decline very quickly. If you're lucky enough to have a traditional larder on a north-facing wall, this will provide ideal conditions for storage. If not, all such perishable items should be kept in the salad drawer of your refrigerator.

Swiftly does it

When it comes to preparation and cooking, speed is of the essence. As soon as you cut into fresh produce, you increase the surface area exposed to oxygen, which begins to destroy vital nutrients. Thus, if you chop potatoes, cabbages, broccoli, spinach or fruit hours before you cook it, you'll be lucky if there is any vitamin C left by the time it is ready to be eaten.

Of course, the way to get maximum nutrition from most fresh produce is to eat it raw or juiced, but following sensible cooking procedures will minimise your loss. I am staggered by the number of people who still add bicarbonate of soda to green vegetables while they are cooking. Yes, it preserves the colour, but it also destroys virtually all traces of vitamin C. Besides, if you don't overcook your greens, they won't end up looking like a grey mess.

Conserve and reserve

Practice conservative cooking practices such as using the least amount of water on vegetables to ensure the shortest possible cooking time; also save that water once the cooking is finished. All vegetable water, in fact, should be kept and used in sauces, soups and gravies, for any nutrients that leach out during the cooking process will remain in the water, and they should not be tipped down the drain.

Cut down on salt

Finally, don't use salt in
cooking if you can possibly
avoid it. The average UK resident
consumes around 12 grams of salt a day;
that's equal to three teaspoons, yet the safe recommended
daily amount is just four grams. Excessive salt intake is a
major factor in the development of high blood pressure, which
in turn is a main cause of heart disease and strokes. Some cardiologists
believe that just halving salt consumption could save up to 100,000 lives a year.

If you're sufficiently interested in your health to be buying organic produce, then
throw away the salt shaker and simply enjoy wonderful, unadulterated flavours.
In addition, remember that three-quarters of our consumption of salt is hidden away in
pre-prepared foods. A bowl of corn flakes, for example, contains more salt than a bowl of
seawater; commercial non-organic bread contains huge amounts of salt. Once you start to
read the labels, you'll find that it crops up in the most unlikely places, but be aware that on
food labels, salt is listed as sodium. To find out how sodium translates into pure salt, multiply
the sodium figure by 2.5. This practice reveals that a modest-sounding 0.8 grams of sodium is
actually two grams of salt – half your safe daily intake.

Preparing organic baby food

Organic food for babies is covered later in this book (*see* page 100), but its preparation merits a
special mention here. Make sure any implements you use are scrupulously clean, and all traces of
washing-up liquid or detergent are completely removed. Use cooled, freshly boiled water if you need
to thin purées. Just as with organic food for adults, do not add salt or sugar to organic baby foods,
either during or after cooking. Never prepare more than enough for two days, and cover and
refrigerate the saved portion as quickly as possible. Anything the baby doesn't eat should be thrown
away. To make life easier, buy a small, stainless-steel mouli grater (cost: around £14 from kitchen
shops) with three different disks. For first foods, use the disk with the smallest holes.

freezing and storing

Organic produce and freezers are a marriage made in heaven. While it is true that freezing destroys some of the vitamin content of produce, this is in fact a slow process and of little health significance – providing the family is also eating plenty of fresh fruits and salads as a general rule.

What to freeze and for how long

The enormous benefit of freezing is that you can take advantage of seasonal gluts when organic produce may well be cheaper than non-organic produce in the supermarket. Beans, peas, peppers, sprouts, soft fruits, sweetcorn... all freeze brilliantly from fresh, and while I may wash or chop them, I never bother with blanching. Just pop the lot into a good-quality freezer bag, and they should keep well for eight to ten months for fruits, ten to twelve months for vegetables. Don't bother thawing, either, when ready to use: simply cook straight from frozen. Apples, pears, plums, damsons, tomatoes and courgettes can be cooked and frozen for later use.

A freezer is also essential if you want to take advantage of organic meats, particularly sausages that don't contain any preservatives; these will keep for two to three months in a freezer, while beef, lamb, pork, duck, goose and rabbit will last for four to six months. Chicken, turkey and venison will keep the longest in a freezer: for ten to twelve months.

Use root vegetables such as carrots and parsnips to make wonderful soups, and freeze a batch for a rainy day. Prepare your own organic tomato sauce, and freeze some for instant pasta dishes. You can even create entire meals such as organic ratatouille – perfect for an evening when you don't want to cook. Fresh herbs can be chopped and frozen in ice cubes, then transferred to plastic bags where they are instantly available for casseroles, soups and sauces.

Conserve and preserve

It's also worth bearing in mind some of the more traditional methods of preserving. You can save a fortune by making your own organic jams, chutneys, pickles and bottled organic fruits; just follow traditional recipes but use organic instead of non-organic ingredients and you'll be amazed at the wealth of colour and flavour you can add to your cupboards. And if you're an organic gardener, you won't need me to tell you what a joy it is to make an organic summer pudding from your own produce to enjoy later at Christmas time.

Buy now, savour later

If you have the space in a cool, frost-free garage (minus the car, of course) or out-building, then it's worth storing other organic crops that can be purchased during their cheapest season. Store beetroot, parsnips and other root vegetables in tea chests full of organic compost (but not the coconut fibre type, as it will influence the taste) or sharp sand; you can also use the compost in the garden when it has served its original purpose. Alternatively, you can store carrots in large vegetable nets – the type used to hold five to ten kilograms of potatoes, for example. Ask your greengrocer for a couple of empty ones.

Store potatoes in old hessian sacks, but make sure you keep them away from light to prevent them from going green and sprouting. Onions, shallots and garlic can be tied in bunches and hung in your garage where they will keep for months. And there is nothing in the world like the smell of a shed or garage in which a few boxes of apples have been stored. Make sure they're not touching each other, and examine them regularly – be certain to remove any that have started to go off. That old adage is true: it takes only one rotten apple to spoil the lot.

The pleasure principle

In the frenetic world we inhabit, it may seem impossible to find time to live in this more traditional way, taking time out to freeze and store organic food almost immediately after you've brought it home. Yet once you start on the organic path – in all of its many aspects – you'll realise that the enormous pleasures derived from these simple tasks, the satisfaction of doing it yourself, and the immeasurable health benefits to you and your family are more than a compensation and make the effort well worthwhile.

Add to this the knowledge that by taking up organic practices you are making a significant contribution to the environment and the world around you, and you'll be amazed at how easy adapting to such traditional tasks becomes. Even your garden benefits, for you can safely add all your vegetable waste and organic storage matter to the compost heap, knowing that there is no risk of contaminating your vegetable patch with someone else's toxic chemicals.

Faced with the choice between unblemished tomatoes, identical in shape, size and colour, and a box of malformed, multicoloured ones with a smell that reminds you of your childhood, which would you choose? Presented with a packet of perfect peppers, would you take them home in preference to gnarled and twisted specimens? Would you instinctively reach for an unblemished, shiny, Red Delicious apple in preference to putting a lacklustre, slightly scabby Cox's Orange into your child's lunch-pack?

food for hea

Because you are reading this book, I hope the answer to all three questions is obvious; beauty, after all, is more than skin deep in produce as well as people. The basic foundation of all naturopathic treatment is that it begins with diet. Diet is the cornerstone that supports optimum health and energy. Your body, mind and spirit all require optimum nutrition, which means taking in every single essential nutrient in its most pure and natural form. This also means avoiding all harmful substances that could damage cells and destroy immunity.

TRACING THE ORGANIC ROLE Organic growing emphasises natural fertilisation of the soil because this ensures the presence of trace minerals such as selenium and zinc, two key substances necessary for the body's conversion of food into energy. These two minerals are found to be lacking in people suffering from chronic fatigue syndrome, myalgic encephalomyelitis (ME) and eating disorders. It is no coincidence that the average intake of both has declined dramatically during the past 20 years.

An organic diet is your only guarantee of optimum nutrition. It is the only certain way of maximising your energy and vitality, and your best chance of resisting the polluted world we live in.

h and energy

FOOD FOR THOUGHT As human beings, we don't live solely on fats, proteins, carbohydrates, vitamins, minerals and enzymes. We live on *food*, food that must smell good and, above all, taste good. Scientists may argue about the relative risks of insecticides, pesticides and food additives that infiltrate our lives, but there can be no argument about flavour.

At the end of the day, no one who has ever tried the organic taste test mentioned on page 10 will have any doubts as to what type of produce tastes best. This is precisely why the vast majority of top chefs I've spoken to would cook with organic produce if ever they were given the choice. And precisely why, in every recipe that follows, it goes without saying that *all* of the ingredients listed should be organic.

This recipe is a real heart protector, since garlic lowers cholesterol, reduces blood pressure and makes blood less likely to clot. It is also excellent for coughs and bronchitis, as garlic also kills the bugs that cause these problems.

spicy
garlic soup

Serves 4

garlic	10 cloves
onion	1 large
olive oil	3 tablespoons, extra virgin
aniseed	1 teaspoon
stale wholemeal bread	2 slices
water	1 litre (35 fl oz)

1 Chop garlic and onion and sweat gently in olive oil until golden. Add aniseed; stir for one minute.

2 Add water, bring to a boil and simmer gently for ten minutes.

3 Add bread and simmer for a further ten minutes, or until the bread has broken down and thickened the soup.

Why choose organic?

Organic produce is more important than ever when making soups. The better nutritional levels in organic soil enriches everything that is grown in it, while the absence of toxic chemicals means that the outer leaves and even skins of vegetables can be used where appropriate, ensuring maximum nutrition as well as value for money.

• 50 calories per 100 g

• Good source of phosphorus, potassium, selenium, folic acid and heart-protective enzymes

If ever there were a liquid mixture of health and energy, this is it. Oats provide slow-release energy as well as a good dose of soluble fibre, which reduces cholesterol levels. Broccoli is packed with heart- and circulatory-protective nutrients in addition to cancer-fighting agents.

organic
celtic broth

Serves 4

olive oil	1 tablespoon, extra virgin
spring onions	5, chopped
broccoli florets	450 g (1 lb)
porridge oats	60 g (2 oz)
vegetable stock and semi-skimmed milk	half and half mix to make 1 litre (35 fl oz)
black pepper	freshly ground to taste
nutmeg	ground to taste
fromage frais	1 tablespoon
chives	1 tablespoon, chopped

1 Pour the oil in a large saucepan and cook spring onions until soft. Add broccoli; stir for two minutes. Add oats, stir for two minutes.

2 Slowly add stock and milk and stir. Cover and simmer gently for 12 minutes.

3 Add pepper and nutmeg to taste and serve with a swirl of fromage frais and a sprinkling of chopped chives.

Why choose organic?

Using organic milk avoids ingesting unwanted antibiotics and hormones. Because they are grown in better-quality soils, organic oats are richer than non-organic oats in the B vitamins essential for the proper maintenance of the nervous system.

• 47 calories per 100 g

• A good source of protein that is low in fat and contains plenty of fibre, calcium, potassium, trace minerals and vitamins A, B and C

The fresh organic pea is a far cry from the shrivelled, tasteless object served in so many restaurants. It is now possible to buy frozen organic peas, too, and they lose little of their extremely valuable nutrients if they are handled properly.

healthy
pea soup

Serves 4

butter	60 g (2 oz)
spring onions	4, chopped
cos lettuce	1 small (or 2 Little Gem lettuces), finely shredded
organic peas,	450 g (1 lb) fresh or frozen
black pepper	freshly ground to taste
water	600 ml (20 fl oz)
fresh mint	1 tablespoon, chopped
crème fraîche	2 tablespoons

1 Melt the butter in a large saucepan, then add onions, lettuce, peas, and pepper. Cover and cook on a low heat for five minutes.

2 Add water and mint, bring slowly to the boil, and simmer for ten minutes.

3 Purée in a blender or food processor, add the crème fraîche, and serve.

Why choose organic?

Peas are a highly nutritious food source – they're particularly important as a protein source for vegetarians – but their food value and flavour are totally dependent upon the nature of the soil in which they are grown. Because organic peas develop in richer soil, they will contain more nutrients and flavour than their non-organic counterparts.

• 70 calories per 100 g

• Rich in protein, providing 15% of the recommended daily requirement per portion

• Supplies more than the daily requirement of thiamine (vitamin B_1), which protects against fatigue, muscle weakness and depression

• Provides half the daily requirement of folic acid, as well as significant amounts of vitamins A, C and E and fibre

Potatoes are at their healthiest and most nutritious when eaten with their skins – something you can do safely only by using organic produce. As well as providing high levels of energy, leeks make this soup a useful treatment for gout, arthritis, rheumatism, chest infections and sore throats.

leek and potato soup

Serves 4

butter	60 g (2 oz)
garlic	1 clove, chopped
leeks	2, chopped
new potatoes	375 g (13 oz), small, unpeeled and unquartered
onion	1 large, sliced
vegetable stock	900 ml (32 fl oz)
fresh parsley	2 tablespoons, finely chopped
black pepper	freshly ground to taste
double cream	150 ml (5 fl oz)

1 Melt the butter in a large saucepan, then sweat the garlic in it for two minutes.

2 Add leeks, potatoes, and onions and cook on a medium heat for ten minutes.

3 Add the stock and simmer for 20 minutes, or until the vegetables are tender.

4 Liquidize in a blender or food processor, then finish by adding parsley, pepper and cream.

Why choose organic?

Only organic potatoes are free from repeated treatments of pesticides and fungicides used to control blight, and they also contain 25% more zinc than their non-organic counterparts. In contrast, commercially grown potatoes receive around eight to ten chemical applications while growing and are then treated again after harvesting to improve their shelf-lives.

• 80 calories per 100 g

• Contains lots of potassium, half the daily requirement of vitamin C, useful amounts of iron, zinc, selenium, iodine, folic acid and beta-carotene, and a healthy contribution of fibre

The combination of the deep, rich yellow of organic eggs and the vivid red and green peppers makes this dish a visual delight as well as a taste sensation. It may take a little longer to make than a conventional omelette, but the result is an energising, sustaining dish. Its roots lie in the peasant cooking of Spain, and, like most peasant food throughout the world, it's delicious, cheap and highly nourishing. With a salad, crusty bread and a glass of wine, what could be better?

free-range
spanish omelette

Serves 4

olive oil	4 tablespoons, extra virgin
potato	1 large, peeled and diced
onion	1 medium, finely sliced
red pepper	half, deseeded, cut in thin strips
courgette	1, unpeeled, sliced thinly
black pepper	freshly ground to taste
eggs	4 free-range, well beaten

Why choose organic?

Organically grown, free-range eggs are free from antibiotics and chemical food additives and any other chemicals fed or injected into non-organically reared birds. Plus, using organic free-range eggs lets you rest easy in the knowledge that you are not subjecting the chickens that produced them to inhumane farming methods.

• 114 calories per 100 g

• Provides a fifth of the recommended daily requirement of protein, lots of potassium, a quarter of daily iodine, and a good supply of folic acid, vitamin C and beta-carotene

• Protects the heart and circulatory system, and helps prevent cancer at the same time

• The sustaining, slow-release energy is good for the entire body, and with just one egg per portion, you needn't worry about cholesterol

1 In a large thick-bottomed frying pan, heat the oil and the potatoes and fry briskly for five minutes, stirring constantly.

2 Turn down the heat, add the onions and cook for five minutes.

3 Add the peppers and cook for four minutes, then add the courgettes and cook for another three minutes until the vegetables are soft (but the onions are not brown).

4 Add freshly ground pepper to the eggs and pour into the pan; turn the heat down and stir thoroughly. Leave the omelette to cook very slowly. As it starts to set, the edge will curl away from the pan.

5 Give the pan a good shake occasionally to keep the omelette moving, and as soon as the underside starts to brown, remove from heat and put under the grill for two to three minutes to finish cooking.

6 Hold a large plate over the frying pan and turn upside down. The omelette should drop out, all in one piece!

Quicker, with fewer calories and easier to make than the traditional Spanish Omelette (opposite), this is a high-protein, mental-energy booster of a dish that takes 15 minutes from cracking the first egg to eating it. Add a wholemeal roll and a piece of fresh fruit, and this becomes fast food with a healthy difference. It's ideal for a light lunch before an afternoon of mental activity and perfect for the weight watchers among you.

gratinée of
courgettes and eggs

Serves 4

olive oil	1 dessertspoon, extra virgin
courgettes	450 g (1 lb) small, well washed and thinly sliced
eggs	4 large, free-range
Red Leicester cheese	2 tablespoons, coarsely grated
sea salt	a tiny pinch
black pepper	freshly ground to taste
chives	1 teaspoon, finely chopped

1 Sauté the courgettes slowly in the oil until they start to brown.

2 Beat the eggs, season and pour over the courgettes. Cook the mixture on a medium heat for a couple of minutes until the bottom sets.

3 Remove from heat; add cheese and put under a hot grill until the cheese begins to brown.

4 Sprinkle with chives before serving.

Why choose organic?

You may not consider courgettes to be nourishing vegetables, but they're very low in calories, good for your skin and rich in folic acid. While most courgettes are not heavily treated with chemicals, some non-organic ones are occasionally treated with fungicides and herbicides, particularly imported varieties, which may have been exposed to more sinister substances such as paraquat. Choose organic courgettes – or better yet, grow your own – and you can eat your fill without anxiety.

• 94 calories per 100 g

• Provides half the daily requirement of folic acid, a fifth of the daily protein requirement and valuable amounts of potassium, iron, selenium and B vitamins

Organic gardener's tip

Grow courgettes together with peas or beans, which put nitrogen into the soil. The courgette repays the favour by using its leaves to cover the earth, preventing weed growth and retaining moisture for all the plants.

It's normal to remove male flowers to encourage the growth of courgettes, but don't throw them away: they're delicious to eat and it's not always easy to get organic ones.

A good Welsh rarebit is a traditional and tasty teatime treat. Some of the best cheesemakers in England, Ireland, Scotland and Wales send their organic farmhouse produce to Randolph Hodgson – the name in the title – at his famous Neal's Yard Dairy, Covent Garden, London.

randolph's
organic rarebit

Serves 4

bread	4 slices, toasted and buttered (sourdough or wholemeal)
butter	for spreading
cheese	90 g (3 oz), organic farmhouse (Lancashire or Cheshire)
sharp fruit chutney	4 teaspoons

Why choose organic?

By using organic cheeses, you avoid accumulated antibiotics which find their way into non-organic cheeses via milk. While the amounts that are passed on to humans are low, there is good evidence to show that this regular low-level intake results in the development of resistant strains of bacteria. In addition, many pesticides are stored in the fat content of non-organic cheese, particularly lindane, a highly toxic chemical that is widely used in many countries.

• 296 calories per 100 g

• Provides loads of protein and plenty of calcium, as well as some iron, lots of selenium, folic acid and 10% of the recommended daily requirement of vitamin E

• Provides a mixture of quick and slow release energy

Courtesy of the Neal's Yard Dairy, Covent Garden, London

Like any simple dish, it is really important to use good ingredients for this recipe. My favourite cheese would be Lancashire or Cheshire, but the bread is important, too. I prefer sourdough, but you could use any bread with good texture and flavour.

– Randolph Hodgson

1 Lightly toast the bread on both sides and spread thinly with butter.

2 Spread each slice with a heaped teaspoon of chutney; slice the cheese finely then crumble on the top of each slice. Pile it high and make sure it comes right to the edges.

3 Place under a hot grill until the cheese is nicely melted. Serve with a simple green salad for a wonderful quick and healthy supper.

This savoury bread pudding takes a few minutes to make, half an hour to cook and is another high-energy lunch or light evening meal. You can vary the flavour by trying any variety of hard organic farmhouse cheese.

cheese and
bread pudding

Serves 4

butter	60 g (2 oz)
wholemeal bread	4 slices, buttered, without crusts
shallots	3, finely chopped
mature Cheddar or Gruyère cheese	175 g (6 oz), grated
eggs	4 medium, free-range
milk	600 ml (20 fl oz)
black pepper	freshly ground to taste
paprika	¼ teaspoon
tomatoes	2, thinly sliced

1 Preheat the oven to 200°C (400°F/gas mark 6).

2 Cut the bread into small squares and place a layer in a buttered pie dish.

3 Make another layer with the shallots, then add the cheese and top with more of the bread.

4 Beat the eggs, milk and pepper, and pour into the dish; sprinkle with paprika.

5 Cover with tomatoes and bake until brown on top (approximately 30 minutes).

Why choose organic?

For reasons to choose organic cheese, *see* page 60. Organic bread is far richer in nutrients than the average non-organic loaf. As well as the multiple applications of chemicals used on non-organic wheat, organophosphates and methyl bromide are widely used after harvesting.

• 160 calories per 100 g

• Provides almost half the daily requirement of protein, well over half the requirement of calcium and vitamin A, and plenty of folic acid

• Lots of iodine, selenium and vitamin C makes this a sustaining, energising and bone-building meal

Organic English lamb is one of the most delicious meats available. Combined with the digestive benefits of mint and the exotic Mediterranean flavour of pine kernels, this ten-minute meal is just as at home on a kitchen table as it is served in a formal dining room. What's more, it will give you plenty of mental energy.

lamb kebabs with pine kernels

Serves 4

lamb	450 g (1 lb) minced
onion	1 medium, peeled and sliced
egg	1 medium, free-range
fresh mint leaves	1 handful, torn
pine kernels	60 g (2 oz)

1 Blend the onion and lamb in a food processor. Add all the other ingredients and run the machine until the mixture is smooth.

2 Divide into four portions and roll each into a long sausage around a kebab stick.

3 Cook under a hot grill until slightly crusty on the outside, turning regularly (about five to six minutes).

4 Serve with slices of unwaxed organic lemon, hot organic wholemeal pita bread and a salad of watercress, mint and chopped spring onions.

Why choose organic?

With less fat than its non-organic relatives, organic lamb is a healthier option right from the start. All meats derived from non-organically managed sources may contain pesticide residues, which are accumulated and stored in animal fats; high amounts have been detected in imports such as New Zealand lamb. Choosing free-range organic lamb also avoids ingestion of any potentially harmful antibiotics and growth hormones.

• 165 calories per 100 g

• Contains only 10% fat (3% of which is saturated)

• Provides half the daily requirement of protein and vitamin E, and masses of iron and zinc

• Provides more than the daily requirement of vitamin B_{12}, and a quarter of a day's supply of folic acid

Ancient Greece was the cradle of bean cuisine. The international crossroads of exotic foodstuffs produced extraordinary combinations – of which this is a prime example. The unique properties of olive oil and dill make this piquant bean dish both delicious and digestible.

byzantine
broad beans

Serves 4

olive oil	2 dessertspoons, extra virgin
broad beans	450 g (1 lb), shelled
spring onions	5, chopped
black pepper	freshly ground to taste
fresh dill	3 tablespoons, chopped
lemons	juice of 2

1 Place oil in a saucepan over medium heat. Add the broad beans, onions and pepper, and sauté for five minutes.

2 Add enough water to cover the beans, and simmer gently for ten minutes.

3 Add the dill and lemon juice, simmer for another ten minutes.

Why choose organic?

While there has been a general reduction in the use of chemicals sprayed on all types of beans, choosing to buy organic broad beans will rule out any contamination from pesticides, herbicides and fungicides – particularly in produce imported from countries where the regulations are not as strict as they should be.

• 55 calories per 100 g

• Provides some protein, plenty of fibre and a good helping of vitamins A and E, potassium and phosphorus

Organic gardener's tip

When you've lifted the last of your potatoes, plant two rows of early broad beans. If the autumn weather is reasonable, you'll be eating your own with Christmas dinner.

A strange but underrated game bird, the guinea fowl looks something like a cross between a turkey, a pheasant and a chicken – but don't let that put you off; it's easy to cook and well worth the effort! It's light and delicious, and here, the intense, aromatic oils from thyme and garlic compete with the sweetness of carrot and the acidity of lemon, the whole dish creating a unique taste experience.

hotpot of
guinea fowl

Serves 4

guinea fowl	1 bird, 1.3 kg (3 lb)
garlic	1 entire head
lemon	½ medium
fresh thyme	1 sprig
olive oil	1 tablespoon, extra virgin
onion	1 medium, sliced
carrots	2 large, cleaned and sliced
black pepper	freshly ground to taste

Why choose organic?

If raised in an organic environment, the bird will be free of growth-promoting chemicals, hormones and antibiotics, and its food won't have been exposed to insecticides, pesticides, herbicides and fungicides. It would not have been forced into such unnatural practices as eating its own kind in the form of pressed pellets. By making sure that all the ingredients in this recipe are organic, you will avoid any chemical residues that may be present in non-organic vegetables.

• 109 calories per 100 g
• Provides full recommended daily requirement of protein
• Rich in phosphorus and potassium
• Contains lots of B vitamins, half the daily requirement of vitamin A
• A great high-protein, low-fat, heart-protective and energy-giving dish

1 Preheat the oven to 180°C (350°F/gas mark 4).

2 Peel all the garlic cloves, cut two of them into thin slivers and slide them under the skin of the guinea fowl, all over the bird. Rub the skin with the lemon and put the sprig of thyme inside the body cavity.

3 Heat the oil in a heavy casserole. Add the onion and carrot and sauté until soft – don't let the onions brown. Remove with a slotted spoon.

4 Add more oil if necessary, then turn up the heat and brown the guinea fowl all over in the casserole.

5 Turn the bird on its back, add the reserved carrots and onions, the rest of the garlic cloves and some black pepper; cover and put in the oven for 40 minutes, or until the juices run clear when the thigh is pricked with a skewer. The onion, garlic and carrots melt down to a rich purée.

6 Remove the bird and cut into quarters. Put a spoonful of purée on each plate and serve a quarter of the bird on top.

The surprising sweet-and-sour flavour of this recipe tempted palates in Eastern Europe long before the appearance of Chinese food in the West. If you have never tasted it, now is the time to sample the real delights of red cabbage.

braised
red cabbage

Serves 4

red cabbage	1 medium
olive oil	2 tablespoons, extra virgin
onion	1 large, chopped
garlic	3 cloves, chopped
cider vinegar	4 tablespoons
brown sugar	1 teaspoon
black pepper	freshly ground to taste

1 Shred the cabbage, rinse well and drain.

2 In a large pan, heat the oil and sweat the onion until soft. Add the garlic, cook for another minute or two, then add the cabbage, stirring until well mixed.

3 Add vinegar, sugar and pepper. Reduce heat, cover and simmer till tender (approximately 30 minutes), stirring occasionally.

Why choose organic?

Most non-organic cabbages are sprayed with organophosphates, which are known to have serious side-effects on the nervous system if ingested in large doses. Non-organic red cabbage is usually sprayed with other fungicides and herbicides, not to mention anti-slug treatments. Because organic cabbages are grown in rich, nutritious soil, they will have a higher food value than their non-organic counterparts.

• 45 calories per 100 g
• Provides a full recommended daily requirement of vitamin C, folic acid and good fibre

Here's another quick and easy recipe that takes ten minutes to prepare and only 20 to cook. Organic rabbit is cheap, extremely low in fat and has been traditional English country fare for centuries.

rabbit
and onions

Serves 4

olive oil	2 tablespoons, extra virgin
rabbit	750 g (1 lb 10 oz), cut into pieces
onion	1 large, finely chopped
tomatoes	4 medium, chopped
dry cider	350 ml (12 fl oz)
fresh parsley	1 handful, chopped
sea salt and	
black pepper	freshly ground to taste

1 In a sauté pan or a large, deep frying pan with a lid, heat the oil and fry the rabbit pieces, stirring well until they're brown all over.

2 Add the onion, and continue to stir for two minutes.

3 Add the rest of the ingredients, cover and simmer for 20 minutes.

Why choose organic?

Organic butchers take pride, time and trouble in the correct storage, hanging and preparation of rabbit, so your produce arrives in peak condition and is perfectly prepared – unlike the plastic-wrapped supermarket version. In addition, you'll know that the animal has been reared and kept under better conditions than its battery farmed counterparts – and that is all without taking the avoidance of chemical residues into consideration.

• Only 105 calories per 100 g

• Very rich in protein, zinc, selenium and vitamin B_{12}, and a valuable source of vitamins B_6, C and E

Many health-conscious people avoid duck thinking that it's high in fat and calories. This simple and quick recipe (30 minutes from start to finish) makes a delightfully light and low-calorie meal, perfect for lunch or late evening when served with wild rice and a tangy shallot and plum tomato salad.

duck breast in
pink pepper sauce

Serves 4

rape-seed oil (canola)	1 tablespoon
duck breasts	4
onion	1 medium, finely chopped
peppercorns (pink)	1 tablespoon
white wine	4 tablespoons, very dry
low-fat crème fraîche	100 ml (4 fl oz)

1 Heat the oil and fry the duck breasts for five minutes on each side till they turn brown. Remove the breasts with a slotted spoon, slice crossways into short, thin strips and keep warm in a serving dish.

2 Fry the onions until just brown, then add the peppercorns and wine. Mix well and simmer for ten minutes.

3 Add the crème fraîche, cook for another two minutes, then pour over the duck.

Why choose organic?

Choosing organically reared duck means avoiding all chemical residues, including antibiotics, which are present in the food (and consequently the meat) of many non-organically reared birds.

- 88 calories per 100 g
- Supplies useful amounts of protein, zinc, iodine and B vitamins, as well as a healthy portion of the valuable mono-unsaturated amino acids

This recipe comes from my favourite fishmonger, David Blagdon, in Marylebone. In spite of fears about ever more polluted oceans, deep-water fish remains one of the healthiest foods in the world – as long as you don't overcook it. Besides tasting great, this dish is a healthy choice due to its low fat content, and thanks to the tomatoes, onions and garlic, it helps prevent heart disease into the bargain.

baked fish with organic tomato, onion and garlic

Serves 4

fresh fish	4 x 175 g (6 oz) fillets: halibut, hake, cod, etc
onion	1 large, finely chopped
tomatoes	4, finely chopped
garlic	2 cloves, finely chopped
olive oil	2 dessertspoons, extra virgin
black pepper	freshly ground to taste

1 Tear off four pieces of aluminium foil large enough to make a loose parcel round each fillet.

2 Mix together the tomato, garlic and onion and spread a layer in the centre of each piece of foil. Put the fish on the mixture and sprinkle what's left on top of each fillet. Season with pepper and a drizzle of the oil.

3 Wrap each into a loose parcel and bake in an oven-proof dish in a preheated oven 200°C (400°F, gas mark 6) for 20 minutes.

Why choose organic?

While traces of pesticides have been detected in most species, fish is still an excellent protein source – much less hazardous to eat than animal protein such as beef or pork. On rare occasions, some farmed salmon and trout contain antibiotic residues, but organophosphates have not been found in them to date.

• 85 calories per 100 g

• Only 7 grams of fat, of which less than 1 gram is saturated

• Provides lots of protein, phosphorus, potassium, folic acid, and useful amounts of minerals, B vitamins and vitamin C

Here's a dessert that tastes good and does you good – a sweet you can eat without feeling guilty. It is quite substantial, however, so save it as a partner for a fairly light meal. As well as loads of energy, this delicious recipe supplies heart-protective pectin, which helps reduce cholesterol. It also offers digestive benefits from the volatile oils present in cloves and cinnamon.

mother's yorkshire pudding with apples

Serves 4

English dessert
apples	450 g (1 lb), crisp
seedless raisins	30 g (1 oz)
soft brown sugar	30 g (1 oz)
cloves	2, whole
ground cinnamon	1 teaspoon
lemon juice	1 tablespoon

Batter:
wholemeal flour	170 g (6 oz)
white flour	60 g (2 oz)
soft brown sugar	90 g (3 oz)
eggs	2 medium, free-range
milk	600 ml (20 fl oz)

1 Layer the peeled, cored and sliced apples on the bottom of a lightly greased oven-proof dish.

2 Add the raisins, lemon juice, sugar and cloves, and sprinkle with cinnamon.

3 Mix together all the batter ingredients, beating thoroughly, and pour over the top.

4 Place in a preheated oven at 170°C (325°F/gas mark 3) and cook for one hour.

Why choose organic?

Organic apples tend to have a much higher vitamin content than non-organic ones. They are also free from the preserving wax used to give non-organic apples a longer shelf-life.

• 120 calories per 100 g

• Provides plenty of protein, fibre, calcium, potassium and vitamin B_{12}, together with useful amounts of iron, zinc, iodine and vitamin E

menus for health and energy

The following sample menus represent healthy, high-energy meals. Obviously, everyone has individual preferences as far as meal planning is concerned, but this guide suggests meals that provide the greatest variety of nutrients in the most balanced proportions.

Although organic produce is now widely available from many supermarkets, specialist shops and by mail order, supplies are not always consistent or guaranteed. Substitute ingredients where necessary, but try to stick to the same group of produce. For example, if the recipe calls for parsnips, use any root vegetable. If peas are specified, then any other member of the legume family will do. For cabbage, substitute kale, spring greens, broccoli, Brussels sprouts, Chinese leaves, pak choi or any available organic brassica.

A Light Lunch or Dinner

- Spicy Garlic Soup (p 54)
- Free-range Spanish Omelette (p 58)
- A mixed green salad
- Fresh fruit

Bursting with antioxidants that protect against heart disease and cancers, this menu is also a good source of energy and provides a powerful boost to the immune system.

A Hearty Traditional Winter Meal

- Leek and Potato Soup (p 57)

- Rabbit and Onions (p 66)

- Mashed swede and carrot

- Steamed broccoli

- Villandry Organic Apple Flans (p 96)

A perfect cold-weather combination that offers protection against colds and sore throats. This meal is rich in complex carbohydrates for energy and warmth, yet it's still low in fat, high in protein and a very good source of fibre.

A Dinner Party with a Healthy Difference

- Grapefruit and orange segments sprinkled with fresh mint leaves

- Hotpot of Guinea Fowl (p 64)

- Braised Red Cabbage (p 65)

- Byzantine Broad Beans (p 63)

- Organic goat's cheese with a stick of crunchy organic celery

This impressive meal is extremely low in fat and overflowing with cancer-fighting phytochemicals. The beans and guinea fowl provide more than the minimum daily requirement of protein, while the meal as a whole offers lots of fibre, plenty of vitamins A, C, and E, loads of B vitamins, potassium, phosphorus and calcium, together with the digestive benefits of fresh mint and dill. To round it off, enjoy with a glass of Fetzer organic red wine from California.

Quick Snack Lunch

- A glass of fresh orange juice

- Randolph's Organic Rarebit (p 60)

- Watercress and finely chopped spring onion salad, drizzled with lemon juice and extra-virgin olive oil

- Natural live yoghurt topped with a spoonful of organic honey and sprinkled with toasted pine kernels

What could be better than this simple, light and highly nourishing menu? It provides masses of immune-boosting vitamin C, half the daily requirement of calcium, plenty of selenium, folic acid, some iron and vitamin E – all this, plus the specific cancer-fighting qualities of watercress, which helps prevent lung cancer.

At certain times of the year, vitality seems to ebb away and natural defences sink. Dark mornings, dark evenings and grey days trigger the aptly named winter blues, giving many people an irresistible desire to binge on treacle tart, steamed puddings and as much chocolate as they can lay their hands on. All too quickly, summer reveals the consequences: the tell-tale bulges, the blotchy skin and endless bad hair days. The merest thought of beaches, swimming costumes and swimming pools fills you with dread.

an organic

DETOXIFY AND REVITALIZE It is at precisely this point that you need to detoxify, or detox, your system. By doing so, you'll boost your vitality, raise your natural defences and eliminate the accumulated waste of months of bad eating, too much drink and not enough exercise. This, of all times, is when organic foods are not an indulgence or luxury, but a vital necessity. You must put only the purest of nutrients into your body to guarantee a super-healing boost to every cell and system.

To be successful, a detox regime must start with a short, sharp fast. The reason? Forty-eight hours of a highly restricted food intake causes unfriendly bacteria to starve to death in your intestines. (This releases toxins, which may cause headaches, but drink plenty of fluids and they'll go away.)

CONSUME FOR IMMUNITY The next step is to begin consuming an abundance of immune-boosting foods. These increase natural resistance to invading bacteria and viruses and will protect you from all manner of infections. Reducing fat to a minimum and increasing the complex carbohydrate portion of the diet also rests the liver and encourages the brain's production of its own "feel-good" chemicals that fight fatigue and depression.

detox regime

For a successful detox regime, avoid meat and be sure to eat foods that supply massive amounts of protective vitamins A, C, and E, beta-carotene, and minerals such as zinc and selenium to prevent heart disease and infections, as well as cancer. Don't ignore the enormous health-giving benefits of fresh organic garlic. If you're cooking garlic, chop it and leave to stand for at least ten minutes before adding to recipes, as this preserves its highly protective chemicals.

The following recipes for simple detox dishes should always be accompanied by fresh organic salads and fruits. Herbal teas and organic juices (preferably home-made) coupled with copious amounts of still mineral water should be your drinks. For a detailed week-long detox plan, *see* pages 80 and 81.

If you're serious about going organic and an occasional detox session, then this recipe is a must. Apart from its wonderful flavour, it has none of the unwanted chemicals present in most stock cubes. Ideally, you need a giant stockpot for the job, but if you don't have one, simply reduce the quantities. Place a large pasta basket inside the pot to hold all the vegetables; it saves straining the stock. This stock freezes brilliantly, especially in ice-cube trays. The cubes can then be put into a large freezer bag, and you can take out as many as necessary for recipes.

vegetable stock

onions	2 large, unpeeled, cut in half
celery	3 sticks with leaves, chopped
carrots	5 large, chopped
turnips	3 medium, chopped
leeks	3 large, chopped (including green part)
garlic	1 entire bulb, unpeeled and halved horizontally
plum tomatoes	3 ripe, quartered
flat-leaf parsley	a generous bunch
thyme, rosemary and bay leaves	a generous bunch, tied together (or 2 bouquet garnis)
peppercorns	5 whole
water	4 litres (135 fl oz)

1 Put all ingredients into the pan, bring to the boil and leave to simmer gently for two hours without a lid.

2 If using a large basket to hold the vegetables, lift it out and use a wooden spoon to press the vegetables in order to extract the maximum flavour and nutrients. If you haven't got a basket, pour through the biggest sieve you have, again using a wooden spoon to squeeze the cooked vegetables. The stock will keep happily in the fridge for several days or for up to three months in the freezer.

Why choose organic?

Because none of the vegetables are peeled, you can only make this stock safely by using organic produce.

- 10 calories per 100 g
- Rich in potassium and vitamin A, with useful quantities of calcium, phosphorus, folic acid, and vitamin C
- Contains beneficial cancer-fighting, heart-protective plant nutrients

Organic gardener's tip

Add the vegetable pulp to the compost heap. All vegetable food waste is ideal for composting, but don't use any meat or fish scraps: they will attract rats as well as passing dogs and cats.

Like cabbage, broccoli and Brussels sprouts, watercress is a brassica – which means it contains natural antibiotics and cancer-fighting phytochemicals. It is also a great cleansing vegetable, known to be specifically protective against lung cancer. Besides tasting great hot, this recipe is equally delicious as a cold summer soup.

watercress soup

Serves 4

garlic	2 cloves, finely chopped
olive oil	1 tablespoon, extra virgin
onion	1 large, finely chopped
curry powder	1 teaspoon
watercress	4 bunches, well washed, with stalks
vegetable stock	900 ml (32 fl oz)
black pepper	freshly ground to taste
plain yoghurt	1 small carton (about 125 ml/4 fl oz), live, low-fat

1 Chop the garlic and leave to stand for ten minutes before cooking. In a large, heavy-bottomed saucepan, heat the oil and cook the onions on a moderate heat until soft and translucent (but not brown).

2 Add the garlic and cook for one minute. Add curry powder, stir continuously and cook for another minute.

3 Turn down the heat; add the watercress and stir and cook until wilted – around two to three minutes.

4 Add the stock and pepper, simmer for ten minutes, then liquidize. Pour into serving bowls and add a spoonful of yoghurt to each.

Why choose organic?

Organically produced watercress is bursting with flavour – particularly that wonderful mustardy, peppery bite that many non-organic versions now lack.

• 25 calories per 100 g

• Very low in fat, 10% of daily iron with modest amounts of iodine, selenium, folic acid and vitamin A

If you're trying to reduce your blood pressure, then aubergines are a must, as they reduce the amount of fat circulating in the arteries. Bulgur wheat, sometimes known as cracked wheat, is often used in place of rice in the Middle East. It's highly nutritious and has a unique nutty flavour. This dish is also great cold, particularly if you add a generous amount of chopped flat-leaf parsley.

aubergine and bulgur stir-fry

Serves 4

bulgur or cracked wheat	250 g (9 oz)
water	475 ml (17 fl oz)
olive oil	6 tablespoons, extra virgin
onions	2 medium, thinly sliced
aubergines	2 large, cut into cubes
ground coriander	3 teaspoons
ground cumin	3 teaspoons
flaked almonds	150g (5½ oz)
raisins	100 g (4 oz)
sea salt	1 pinch
black pepper	freshly ground to taste

1 In a large saucepan, simmer the bulgur wheat covered in the water for ten minutes, or until most or all of the water has been absorbed and the grains are soft and tender. Drain if necessary.

2 Heat the oil and fry the onions until brown. Add the aubergines and, stirring frequently, sauté until brown (add extra oil if necessary, since the aubergine acts like a sponge). Add the spices to the pan and cook for one minute, stirring constantly.

3 Lower the heat and add the flaked almonds and raisins and brown slightly. Stir the cooked bulgur wheat into the vegetables, add extra oil and sauté for one minute to heat through. Season to taste and serve immediately.

Why choose organic?

Using organic raisins not only avoids any agrochemical residues but also the mineral oil that is normally applied to commercial dried fruits.

• 320 calories per 100 g

• A good source of protein, fibre, potassium, iron, selenium and folic acid

• Also provides more than the daily requirement of vitamin E, and modest amounts of A and C

• The high fibre content stimulates the digestive system, making this a very useful detox dish

Unlike other cereals, buckwheat doesn't contain gluten, the sticky proteins present in cereal grains. However, it is rich in rutin, a substance that strengthens the tiniest blood vessels in the circulatory system. This is a really satisfying and cleansing dish with the added bonus of the beneficial live bacteria from the yoghurt. You can find buckwheat at most health-food shops and also in some supermarkets.

mushrooms with egg and buckwheat

Serves 4

buckwheat	225 g (8 oz) whole grains
egg	1 large, free-range
butter	60 g (2 oz)
sea salt	1 pinch
boiling water	450 ml (16 fl oz)
onion	1 large, finely chopped
olive oil	1 tablespoon, extra virgin
mushrooms	225 g (8 oz), thinly sliced
coriander leaves	1 tablespoon, chopped
black pepper	freshly ground to taste
plain yoghurt	1 small carton (about 125 ml/4 fl oz), live, low-fat

Why choose organic?

Non-organic cereal grains are often grown in "dust bowl" areas by intensive monocropping of vast acreage.

• 123 calories per 100 g

• Provides 9 grams of protein, lots of carbohydrates, fibre, plenty of potassium, and valuable amounts of iron, zinc, copper, selenium, iodine, vitamin B$_6$, folic acid and vitamin A

• A great detoxifier, as it stimulates digestive function as well as relieving varicose veins, high blood pressure and hardening of the arteries

1 Boil the buckwheat for 15 minutes until soft.

2 Beat the egg in a large bowl and add the buckwheat, stirring thoroughly. Put the mixture in a non-stick (but ungreased) pan and stir slowly over a low heat until toasted and dry.

3 Use a little of the butter to grease an oven-proof dish. Put in the buckwheat, the rest of the butter, a pinch of salt and the boiling water. Preheat oven to 180°C (350°F/gas mark 4) and bake for 20 minutes.

4 While the buckwheat bakes, sweat the onions in the oil until they're soft, but not brown. Add the mushrooms and cook for another five minutes. Add the coriander and pepper, stirring constantly.

5 When the buckwheat is done, stir in the onion and mushroom mixture, add the yoghurt and serve hot.

This is a super-easy and very quick recipe that exploits the wonderful texture and flavour of organic chicken. The garlic and paprika give this dish the unmistakable tang of Hungary and combine the detoxifying properties of garlic with the circulatory stimulus of paprika.

grilled
paprika chicken

Serves 4

olive oil	2 tablespoons, extra virgin
lemon	1 large (juice and grated rind)
garlic	2 cloves, smashed, not chopped
paprika	1 generous teaspoon
black pepper	freshly ground to taste
chicken breasts	4 medium, skinned and cut into large cubes

1 Combine the oil, lemon juice and zest, garlic, paprika and pepper in a shallow dish. Put the chicken cubes in the marinade and stir well to make sure they are all coated. Leave in the fridge for half an hour, but spoon the marinade over the chicken at least twice during that time.

2 Brush the rack of a grill pan with oil. Lift the chicken pieces out of the marinade with a slotted spoon, place on the rack and grill on a high temperature for ten minutes, turning occasionally and basting with the marinade.

Why choose organic?

Not only does organic poultry taste infinitely superior, it is your only guarantee that the meat contains no unwanted chemical residues.

• 175 calories per 100 g

• Provides large amounts of protein, phosphorus, potassium and lots of selenium

• A low-fat, heart-friendly dish (only one gram of saturated fat per 100 grams) which stimulates the circulation and provides slow-release energy

Here's a second quick recipe that spares you the antibiotics and chemical residues that will almost certainly be present in non-organic poultry. The antiseptic properties of thyme and the cancer-fighting effects of essential oils in the lemon make this dish exceptionally healthy as well as cleansing.

organic sicilian chicken

Serves 4

wholemeal flour	3 tablespoons
dried thyme	2 teaspoons
sea salt	ground to taste
black pepper	freshly ground to taste
chicken thighs	8 medium
milk	100 ml (3½ fl oz)
olive oil	4 tablespoons, extra virgin
lemon	juice of 1

1 Preheat the oven to 190°C (375°F/gas mark 5). Mix together the flour, thyme and seasoning. Dip the chicken pieces in milk, then coat thoroughly with the flour mixture; set aside.

2 Heat the oil in a frying pan, and fry the chicken on all sides until golden brown. Transfer to a wire tray placed over a baking sheet.

3 Pour the lemon juice over the chicken pieces and bake in an oven-proof dish for 15 minutes. Can be served hot or cold.

Why choose organic?

See Grilled Paprika Chicken, opposite

• 200 calories per 100 g

• Provides half the minimum daily requirement of protein, more than 10% of calcium, a third of iron and selenium, and a little of all the B vitamins

a seven-day organic detox diet

My patients have used this seven-day detox regime with great success. Be warned, however: the first day is tough, and you'll probably have a headache, but after that it's plain sailing.

DAY 1: 600 calories

A real fasting day, so choose a time when you can get plenty of rest.

Breakfast, lunch, dinner: 1 glass of unsweetened organic fruit or vegetable juice. 1 small carton of live low-fat natural yoghurt. Drink at least 5 pints of still mineral water or herbal teas (don't use milk, but you can add half a teaspoon of organic honey).

DAY 2: 1,200 calories

Standard breakfast: (To eat throughout the week) 1 portion fresh fruit (vary throughout the week): apple, pear, mango, grape, pineapple or grapefruit. 2 slices of wholemeal toast spread with low-fat cottage cheese. 1 small carton of live low-fat yoghurt. A small glass of skimmed milk.
A cup of herbal or weak Indian tea without milk or sugar.

Lunch: 1 kiwi fruit. 200 g (7 oz) mixed raw vegetable salad: a bed of lettuce filled with grated carrot, celeriac and raw beetroot, with a squeeze of lemon juice and a drizzle of olive oil. 170 g (6 oz) of any steamed vegetables, sprinkled with a chopped garlic clove and a drizzle of olive oil.
Herbal or weak Indian tea.

Dinner: 60 g (2 oz) organic berries in 120 g (4 oz) unsweetened organic muesli mixed with the juice of an orange and a small carton of live low-fat yoghurt. Herbal or weak Indian tea.

DAY 3: 1,100 calories

Standard breakfast

Lunch: 1 large mango. 170 g (6 oz) mixed salad (watercress, fresh mint, spring onions, tomato, red/yellow peppers, chicory, baby spinach, bean sprouts), with lemon juice and olive oil dressing. 1 large jacket potato (with skin) with 60 g (2 oz) low-fat fromage frais, whipped with chopped chives and a clove of garlic. Glass of vegetable juice.

Dinner: 1 small carton of live low-fat yoghurt with mixed berries and a teaspoon of honey. 1 crusty wholemeal roll with a matchbox-size piece of soft organic cheese: brie, camembert, or similar. Herbal or weak Indian tea.

DAY 4: 800 calories

Your main food today will be organic rice, traditionally used by naturopaths as a cleansing treatment. Make enough for the entire day: 100 g (3½ oz) dry brown rice cooked in a pint of water (or half water and half vegetable stock for a more savoury flavour). Drink only water (at least five pints) with meals and in between.

Breakfast: 85 g (3 oz) rice with 145 g (5 oz) stewed apple and honey, cinnamon and grated lemon rind.

Lunch: 85 g (3 oz) rice with 200 g (7 oz) steamed vegetables: celery, leek, carrot, tomato, spinach, broccoli and shredded cabbage.

Dinner: 85 g (3 oz) rice mixed with soaked dried apricots, raisins, sultanas, and the flesh of a pink grapefruit.

DAY 5: 1,100 calories

Standard breakfast

Lunch: 1 apple. 1 pear. 170 g (6 oz) raw vegetable salad (cauliflower and broccoli florets, carrot, spring onion, grated red cabbage, mange tout) tossed in olive oil and cider vinegar dressing, sprinkled with a teaspoon of raisins, and 3 chopped Brazil nuts.
1 large jacket potato (with skin) filled with 85 g (3 oz) steamed spinach, chopped, with 2 teaspoons of olive oil, a chopped garlic clove and a generous grating of nutmeg.
Herbal or weak Indian tea.

Dinner: 85 g (3 oz) fromage frais mixed with a carton of live, low-fat yoghurt, poured over a generous bowl of mixed fruit salad, including kiwi, pineapple, orange, grapes, berries and apple.
Herbal or weak Indian tea.

DAY 6: 1,300 calories

Standard breakfast

Lunch: 1 banana. 170 g (6 oz) mixed salad: mixed shredded lettuce leaves (Cos, little gem, lamb's lettuce, radicchio), tomato, olives, red pepper, carrot, spring onions, cucumber, a clove of garlic, fennel and watercress, with a dressing of lemon juice, walnut oil and tarragon. 1 large jacket potato filled with 85 g (3 oz) steamed French or runner beans sprinkled with a dessertspoon of sunflower oil and finely chopped onions.
Herbal or weak Indian tea.

Dinner: 85 g (3 oz) muesli mixed with a dessertspoon of lemon juice, a teaspoon of honey, grated apple and a small carton of live low-fat yoghurt. 1 slice wholemeal bread, with a matchbox-sized piece of brie, camembert or similar soft organic cheese. 1 slice wholemeal bread with honey.
Herbal or weak Indian tea.

DAY 7: 1,200 calories

Standard breakfast

Lunch: 170 g (6 oz) mixed salad (watercress, baby spinach, mixed lettuce leaves, parsley, celery, garlic, chives, basil, tomato) with a dressing of ⅓ walnut oil, ⅓ olive oil, ⅓ cider vinegar and a teaspoon of Dijon mustard (make a large amount and store in bottles), sprinkled with sunflower seeds.
85 g (3 oz) boiled potatoes in their skins.
One trout stuffed with finely chopped parsley, onion, tomato and pine nuts, covered in thinly sliced lemon, baked in foil with a little olive oil.
Vegetarian alternative: stir-fried tofu with shredded carrot, bean sprouts, mange tout and soy sauce OR a grilled veggie-burger.
A glass of dry white wine.

Dinner: 1 whole pink grapefruit.
2 poached eggs on two slices of wholemeal toast with a scrape of butter.
Herbal or weak Indian tea.

Well done! If you haven't cheated, you're probably four or five pounds lighter, your eyes are bright, your skin is clear and you feel terrific. The high-fibre content of this week has really got your digestion working and all the super-protective natural chemicals in pure, unadulterated organic food have lifted your spirits. Best of all, you'll finish the week with lower blood pressure, less cholesterol and a rested liver.

Taking some exercise is also vital to a detox regime. No matter what the weather, dress appropriately and get into the fresh air and daylight whenever possible. Even on overcast days, you'll get enough sunlight to help ward off the problems of seasonal affective disorder syndrome (SADS). A brisk, 20-minute walk three times a week will make all the difference.

There will never be a more critical period in your child's life in which to avoid exposure to damaging substances than during pregnancy. Even if the levels of chemical residue in non-organic foods are very small, if they get into you, they will get into your developing baby – and minute doses of toxic chemicals could be potentially devastating to a developing foetus. Crop residues are not the only problem. Illegal growth hormones have been discovered in meat purchased from butchers' shops throughout

food for a heal

the EU. Excessive levels of antibiotics have been found in dairy products, and may cause the development of resistant strains of bacteria in babies and young children.

None of these problems occur in organic food. What's even more reassuring is that not a single case of mad cow disease has been documented in cattle bred and raised on wholly organic farms. Do you need more reasons for starting yourself, your partner and your developing child on an organic path?

THE THREE-MONTH RULE That path begins long before the baby does – three months before conception, in fact, when prospective mothers and (ideally) fathers should be feeding themselves organically. This may sound surprising, but it gives your baby the greatest chance of growing and developing healthily in the womb. By doing so, he or she can come into this world in the best possible condition to survive, thrive and enjoy a healthy childhood.

THE RIGHT DIET The optimum diet before and during pregnancy contains a wide variety of organic wholefoods. Wholegrain cereals, along with plenty of carbohydrate-rich bread, pasta, brown rice, potatoes and beans, should contribute at least

ny pregnancy

50 per cent of your daily calorie intake. Next, you'll need good oils: olive oil, sunflower oil and modest amounts of animal fat from dairy products and animal protein. No more than 33 to 35 per cent of your calories should come from all fats, with a maximum of ten per cent from saturated fat.

Protein should make up only around 12 per cent of your total daily calories. Before and during pregnancy, mothers should take in half their protein from oily fish, as essential fatty acids in fish foster good foetal brain development.

Embarking on an organic lifestyle shows a concern for your unborn child, yourself, your partner and the environment. Little wonder, then, that ancient Chinese physicians would have called it *Té Tao* – "The Way to Virtue".

Here's a perfect pregnancy soup with virtually no saturated fat, plenty of carbohydrates to keep you going and all the circulatory benefits of garlic to protect against varicose veins. It's quick and easy to make, and if you really can't be bothered, you don't even have to peel the tomatoes. What's more, this soup provides an ideal balance of nutrients for you and the baby.

fresh
tomato soup

Serves 4

olive oil	2 tablespoons, extra virgin
onion	1 medium, finely chopped
garlic	3 cloves, chopped
tomatoes	750 g (1 lb 10 oz), peeled and quartered
vegetable stock	900 ml (32 fl oz; *see* p 74)
stale wholemeal bread	3 thick slices, crusts removed
black pepper	freshly ground to taste
plain yoghurt	1 small carton (about 125 ml/4 fl oz), live, low-fat
chives	1 small bunch

1 Heat the oil in a large, heavy-bottomed saucepan. Add the onion and cook gently for two or three minutes until soft. Add the garlic and cook for another two minutes, but do not brown.

2 Add the tomatoes and cook gently until they fall apart. Add the vegetable stock, cook for another five minutes, then break the bread into the mixture. Cook for a further three minutes, then season with black pepper. For the fullest flavour, serve tepid with a swirl of yoghurt and a sprinkle of finely chopped chives.

Why choose organic?

Tomatoes that are organically grown offer much better flavour, aroma and nutritional quality.

• 46 calories per 100 g

• Provides 10% of the minimum daily protein requirement, valuable amounts of selenium, niacin, folic acid, vitamins A, C and E, and masses of heart-protective lycopene

Organic gardener's tip

Plant tomatoes beside the asparagus bed, with parsley sown between each tomato plant. This helps deter unwanted pests.

Enjoy the legendary benefits of onions now, before it's time to breastfeed; some babies don't like them! Onions are powerfully antibiotic and protect against infections, and give this soup the power to detoxify and cleanse. They also lower cholesterol levels and reduce the risk of blood clots. What more could a mother-to-be ask for?

french
onion soup

Serves 4

olive oil	1 tablespoon, extra virgin
onions	3 large, sliced
potato	1 medium, peeled and diced
vegetable stock	900 ml (32 fl oz; *see* p 74)
black pepper	freshly ground to taste
fresh thyme	1 sprig
fresh lemon juice	2 teaspoons

Optional:

wholemeal French bread	8 slices .
Gruyère cheese	115 g (4 oz), coarsely grated

1 Heat the oil in a large, heavy-bottomed saucepan and sweat the onions until they just start to turn brown.

2 Add the potato, stock, pepper, thyme and lemon juice; bring to the boil and simmer gently for 20 minutes.

3 To enjoy this soup as they do in France, float two slices of wholemeal French bread on the top, sprinkle with grated organic Gruyère cheese and place under a hot grill until the cheese melts.

Why choose organic?

Organic onions have a higher content of the enzyme allinase, which releases the equally higher content of sulphurous compounds; these not only make you cry but give onions their flavour – which is why organic onions are much stronger than their non-organic relatives.

• Including the bread and cheese: 65 calories per 100 g

• Provides a quarter of your protein, lots of fibre and important amounts of calcium, magnesium, potassium, selenium and folic acid

Another great pregnancy soup that offers very little fat, lots of energy and body-building nutrients for both you and the baby. Nothing is lost through cooking, and the combined circulatory benefits of onions, beetroot and pectin from the apple juice are a major health boost.

beet-treat soup

Serves 4

beetroot	500 g (1 lb 2 oz), uncooked, peeled and grated
onion	1 medium, finely chopped
apple juice	600 ml (20 fl oz), unfiltered
lemon juice	1 teaspoon
black pepper	freshly ground to taste
sour or single cream	150 ml (5 fl oz)

1 Place the onions and beetroot in a food processor, together with a cupful of the apple juice; blend until smooth.

2 Stir in the rest of the juice, add pepper and chill. Serve in glass bowls (for maximum effect!) with a swirl of cream.

Why choose organic?

Non-organic beets are risky business as they are treated with fungicides, herbicides and insecticides, especially dichloropropene and malathion; also sometimes lindane.

• 54 calories per 100 g

• Provides very little fat but masses of potassium, folic acid and vitamin C, and useful amounts of iron and vitamin A

This very simple, uncooked dressing uses the dazzling flavours of prime-quality organic fruits and vegetables in season for a pure yet gutsy flavour. It needs to be made a day beforehand, and is best served just warm to bring out all the flavours. Light yet versatile, it is superb served in the early autumn when the tomatoes are at their best. Try it with a roast fillet of cod studded with garlic and prosciutto.

tessa's own tomato and olive oil dressing

fresh bay leaves	4
fresh chives	a handful
garlic	3 fat cloves
plum tomatoes	18 very ripe
red pepper	1 medium
fresh parsley	6 stalks, torn
fresh basil	5 large sprigs, torn
lemon	2 strips of zest
olive oil	600 ml (20 fl oz), extra virgin
white wine vinegar	55 ml (2 fl oz)
coarse sea salt	1 pinch
peppercorns (black)	1 teaspoon, crushed
demerara sugar	4 teaspoons

Why choose organic?

Chemical residues have been found in more than half the UK-produced tomatoes and in 60% of imported crops.

• 336 calories per 100 g

• Provides vitamin A, C and E, folic acid, B vitamins, and plenty of potassium

• Valuable for its heart-protective and cancer-fighting lycopenes from the tomatoes, the calming benefits of basil and the gentle diuretic action of parsley

I like to use organic ingredients because I can be sure of their quality, provenance and flavour – and it shows.

– Tessa Bramley, chef-patron, the Michelin-starred Old Vicarage Restaurant, Ridgeway, near Sheffield

1 Tear the bay leaves in half and tear the chives into pieces. Peel and chop the garlic.

2 Remove seeds from tomatoes and roughly chop the flesh. Remove core, seeds and membrane from pepper and roughly chop flesh.

3 Place all ingredients in a large bowl and press together with the back of a ladle to release the juices and flavours. Leave in fridge overnight for flavours to infuse.

4 Press through a coarse sieve, using the back of a ladle to force through as much of the pulp as possible. Adjust seasoning if necessary.

5 Heat gently and whisk well to emulsify before serving.

A bone-building dish for mother and baby, this recipe is quick and easy to make as well as delicious. It makes a light and, thanks to the coriander, easily digestible meal with abundant baby-friendly nutrients.

wild mushroom and radicchio salad

Serves 4

field mushrooms	12
olive oil	3 tablespoons, extra virgin
garlic	2 cloves, finely chopped
radicchio	1 medium
plum tomatoes	6, thinly sliced
parmesan	a generous pile of thin slivers
coriander	a handful, coarsely chopped
black pepper	freshly ground to taste

1 Brush the mushrooms clean but don't wash them. Heat the oil in a large frying pan, add the garlic and, after one minute, add the mushrooms, cooking them on both sides for three or four minutes.

2 Layer four plates with the radicchio and a ring of tomato slices. Place three mushrooms in the centre of each, pour over a drizzle of the garlic-flavoured oil, and add the parmesan slivers.

3 Sprinkle with coriander and black pepper – and serve.

Why choose organic?

Wild or field mushrooms from organic sources are the most delicious and nutritious available.

• 130 calories per 100 g

• Provides plenty of protein, calcium, potassium, vitamins A, C and E, and folic acid, together with some selenium, iodine and B vitamins

Organic potatoes cooked within minutes of harvesting are one of the world's great taste treats – and here's a way to show them off at their best, as recommended by one of England's most innovative cookery writers. "Organic produce is great," says Josceline Dimbleby. "I can enjoy food more when I'm not doing myself any harm – only a lot of good to both body and spirit."

josceline's
ultimate potato salad

Serves 4

new potatoes	750 g (1 lb 10 oz)
anchovy fillets	in olive oil, 1 can, 50 g (2 oz)
double cream	150 ml (5 fl oz)
natural yoghurt	2 tablespoons, full-fat
black pepper	freshly ground to taste
fresh chives	a generous bunch, finely chopped

Why choose organic?

Non-organic potatoes are treated heavily throughout their growing cycles with repeated applications of insecticides, herbicides and fungicides.

• 137 calories per 100 g

• Provides useful amounts of protein, fibre, calcium, potassium, iodine, folic acid and vitamin B_{12}, also good quantities of vitamins A and C

• For pregnant women, the bonus is the essential Omega-3 fatty acids from the anchovies – essential for development of the baby's brain and central nervous system

Organic gardener's tip

Plant horseradish near your potatoes to deter insects and blight.

1 Wash the potatoes and scrub off as much of the skin as you can but do not peel them. Cut any larger potatoes in half. Either steam or boil until they are cooked, drain and transfer them to a mixing bowl.

2 Empty the anchovy fillets and their oil into the top of a double boiler, or into a bowl set over a saucepan of simmering water. Stir constantly until the anchovies melt down into a smooth mixture.

3 Pour the cream into a saucepan, bring to the boil and bubble for three to four minutes until it thickens slightly, stirring constantly.

4 Remove the cream from the heat and stir in the smooth anchovy mixture; leave to cool.

5 Stir in the yoghurt and season to taste with black pepper (salt isn't necessary because of the salty anchovies). Finally, stir the chopped chives into the creamy mixture, then pour onto the potatoes. Mix well.

Pasta is good at any time, but especially so during pregnancy. Wholemeal pasta contains fibre and B vitamins, so choose your favourite – as long as it's organic. Nearly all organic cheeses are made by small traditional cheesemakers, so the quality and flavour of this parmesan is superb. Combined with the fresh, clean flavours of courgette, it provides a delicious and healthy, easy-to-cook meal.

pasta organic with raw courgette

Serves 4

olive oil	1 teaspoon, extra virgin
salt	a couple of pinches
spaghettini	450 g (1 lb)
courgettes	200 g (7 oz) washed, unpeeled, finely grated
butter	10 g (⅓ oz)
fresh parmesan	2 tablespoons, finely grated
black pepper	freshly ground to taste

1 Add the olive oil and salt to a large saucepan full of water and bring to the boil.

2 Add the pasta and stir for a few seconds to avoid sticking.

3 Fill a serving dish with boiling water to warm it.

4 When the pasta is cooked, drain. Empty the water from the serving dish; put in the pasta, add the courgette, butter, parmesan and pepper and mix thoroughly.

Why choose organic?

The nutritional value of organically produced, unpasteurised milk is inevitably higher, so organic cheeses have higher calcium and protein values.

• 108 calories per 100 g

• A good source of protein, fibre, folic acid, and energy, together with useful amounts of vitamins A and C

Here's a complete meal in under half an hour. Bulgur wheat gives this dish a very different texture and flavour to rice, and it offers all the heart and circulatory benefits of onions and garlic into the bargain. Serve it in the traditional Middle Eastern way, with yoghurt, onions and a green salad.

complete
eastern risotto

Serves 4

butter	60 g (2 oz), unsalted
onion	1 large, finely chopped
garlic	2 cloves, chopped
bulgur wheat	250 g (9 oz)
chicken or **vegetable stock**	450 ml (16 fl oz)
sea salt	1 pinch

Garnish:

onion	1 large, sliced into rings
peanut or **rape-seed oil**	1 tablespoon
plain yoghurt	1 small carton (about 125 ml/4 fl oz), live, full-fat

1 Over a low heat, melt the butter in a large, heavy-bottomed saucepan. Add the chopped onion and garlic and cook gently until they start changing colour.

2 Add the wheat and stir until coated with butter.

3 Add enough stock to cover the mixture, add a pinch of salt, bring to the boil, cover and simmer gently for ten minutes, or until the liquid is absorbed (add more stock if it seems to be drying out too quickly).

4 While the bulgur is cooking, fry the onion rings till they begin to crisp. Serve the bulgur decorated with onion rings and yoghurt.

Why choose organic?

Like its relatives onions, spring onions and leeks, non-organic garlic is most heavily treated with herbicides and fungicides.

• 185 calories per 100 g

• Good carbohydrate dish with plenty of protein, fibre, iodine and vitamin A, and useful amounts of iron, vitamin B_1, niacin and folic acid

The lower fat content and firmer texture of the flesh put wild salmon in a completely different league to its farmed, less flavourful cousin. The peppery bite of watercress and the crunch of wholegrain mustard are what give this dish an even more distinctive flavour.

wild salmon moutarde

Serves 4

olive oil	4 tablespoons extra virgin
onion	1 medium, finely chopped
dry white wine	60 ml (2 fl oz)
sea salt	a pinch
black pepper	freshly ground to taste
wholegrain mustard	2 tablespoons
watercress	1 bunch
salmon steaks	4 thick ones
lemon	1 medium, unwaxed

1 Whisk the oil, onion, wine, salt, pepper and mustard until thoroughly mixed. Pour into a flat, shallow dish and add the steaks, turning two or three until they are well coated. Refrigerate for about three hours, turning and basting a few times.

2 Brush a little oil onto the rack of your grill pan. Put the salmon steaks on the rack and pour over a little of the marinade. Grill on high for four minutes, turn, add more marinade and cook the other side.

3 Serve with watercress and a slice of lemon.

Why choose organic?

In theory, fish farming should be fine, but in practice the fish may be fed artificial colourings, anti-fungal and antibiotic drugs, and their flesh may contain less of the essential fatty acids than in their wild counterparts.

• 215 calories per 100 g

• Provides masses of protein and healthy mono-unsaturated fat, lots of phosphorus, potassium, selenium, iodine, folic acid and vitamins D and E, and four day's worth of vitamin B_{12}

• Also provides generous amounts of essential Omega-3 fatty acids

When you're starting with the wonderful flavour and texture of a free-range organic chicken, you may ask why it's cooked with so much garlic. In truth, the gentle flavours of garlic permeate through the chicken, which ends up with a remarkably mild, garlicky flavour. Its lower fat content means you get a highly nutritious dish, oozing with flavour and valuable medicinal properties.

finger-lickin'
free-range chicken

Serves 4

olive oil	3 tablespoons, extra virgin
butter	a walnut-sized knob, unsalted
sea salt	to taste
black pepper	freshly ground to taste
chicken	4 leg quarters
garlic	at least 10 large, unpeeled cloves
dry white wine	300 ml (10 fl oz)
parsley and coriander	a generous tablespoon of chopped mixed leaves

Why choose organic?

As with all free-range organic animals, your chicken will have a much lower fat content than the factory-farmed equivalent – not to mention a much higher-quality life before it got to you.

• 137 calories per 100 g

• Provides nearly a whole day's protein, useful amounts of magnesium, potassium, iron, zinc, selenium, iodine, vitamin B$_{12}$ and folic acid.

• A valuable recipe in pregnancy, as the powerful antibiotic and antifungal substances in garlic offer protection from all manner of infections. It also helps control cholesterol and blood pressure and reduces the risk of blood clots.

1 The best way to cook this dish is in a traditional straight-sided fricassee pan, otherwise you'll need a large, deep frying pan. Heat the oil and butter together, put lots of black pepper and a pinch of sea salt on the chicken pieces and brown them well, about five minutes each side.

2 Lower the heat, add the garlic cloves, pushing them under the chicken and fry gently for another ten minutes, shaking the pan to keep the chicken moving.

3 Add the wine, and scrape loose all the delicious, crunchy pieces that have stuck to the pan. Leave on the heat for another ten minutes until the chicken is completely cooked through.

4 Place each portion on a plate and arrange the garlic cloves around it, sprinkle with the parsley and coriander, and enjoy with homemade organic wholemeal bread (*see* p 106) and a glass of white wine.

Organic free-range lamb is one of the great flavour sensations of English cooking. Naturally reared, and free from antibiotics, hormones, pesticides and insecticides, these animals will have grazed on natural pastures – a practice that produces much fuller natural flavours. Combined with the oriental tang of garlic, ginger and sesame oil, the result is a delicious dish that is very low in fat but rich in nutrients.

oriental
lamb stir-fry

Serves 4

lamb	450 g (1 lb), lean, cut in thin strips
dry sherry	1 dessertspoon
soy sauce	1 dessertspoon
sesame oil	1 teaspoon
olive oil	1 tablespoon, extra virgin
leek	1 small, washed and sliced in 5-cm (2-inch) long thin slivers
spring onions	2 medium, chopped, including green tops
garlic	2 cloves, chopped
ginger root	25 g (1 oz), peeled and grated

1 Remove every scrap of fat from the lamb. Place in a shallow dish with the sherry, soy sauce and sesame oil. Marinate for half an hour, spooning the marinade over the lamb two or three times.

2 Heat a wok or large frying pan. Add olive oil, lamb and some of the marinade and stir-fry for four minutes. Add the rest of the ingredients and stir-fry for another two or three minutes.

Why choose organic?

Antibiotics are a major concern in non-organic meat; they're often fed automatically as growth promoters and used illegally and indiscriminately for the treatment of illness in non-organic animal husbandry.

• 148 calories per 100 g

• Provides lots of protein, iron, zinc, selenium, iodine, and B vitamins, especially B_{12} and folic acid; also some of vitamins A, C and E

• Ginger helps prevent nausea and indigestion, while the soy sauce provides some natural cancer-fighting elements.

Joe Collier is one of few butchers allowed to buy organic beef from Prince Charles' estate at Highgrove. Eastwoods is his wonderful organic butcher's shop in Berkhamstead, where you can hardly see the walls for certificates and medals. After trying this carnivore's delight, with its rich, mushroomy flavours, you'll understand why. With its wide range of nutrients, this is a super meal for mums-to-be.

joe's organic highgrove beef

Serves 6 to 8

beef rib-eye	1 kilo (approx 2 lbs)
breadcrumbs	120 g (approx 4 oz)
mushrooms	60 g (2 oz) (chanterelles are best)
sausage meat	60 g (2 oz) (use an egg if you prefer)

1 Preheat oven to 220°C (425°F/gas mark 7).

2 In a mixing bowl, combine breadcrumbs, mushrooms and sausage meat (or egg).

3 Cut a pocket in the rib-eye. Put the stuffing into the beef and secure with string. Check the weight, place in a roasting tin and put into the oven.

4 After ten minutes, reduce temperature to 200°C (400°F/gas mark 6) and continue cooking for 15 minutes per 450 g (1 lb).

Why choose organic?

There hasn't been a single case of BSE in cattle bred and raised on an organic farm, so you can eat this dish without worrying. What's more, it won't contain antibiotics, growth hormones or traces of any of the hundreds of agrochemicals that could possibly harm your baby.

• 284 calories per 100 g

• Provides a whole day's protein, zinc, niacin, vitamin B_{12}, and useful amounts of folic acid and other B vitamins

Villandry is one of my favourite food shops in London and must be one of the best in the country. Rosie, the proprietor's wife, gave me this recipe as it's one I love to eat at their restaurant. Made with luscious organic apples and free-range organic eggs, it's a scrumptious, indulgent yet healthy treat – even when you're pregnant.

villandry organic apple flans

Serves 6

caster sugar	200 g (7 oz)
water	60 ml (2 fl oz)
organic dessert apples	1200 g (2 lb 10 oz)
granulated sugar	2 tablespoons
lemon	grated rind from 1, unwaxed
eggs	7 free-range (5, plus 2 yolks)

1 Preheat oven to 180°C (350°F/gas mark 4).

2 In a saucepan over low heat, melt the caster sugar and water together to make a caramel and pour into six ramekins, brushing it around the sides.

3 Peel, chop and gently cook apples until soft. Add two tablespoons sugar and the lemon rind. Beat eggs and yolks lightly and add them to the apple mixture.

4 Fill ramekins, put into a bain-marie, cover with foil and bake for 40 minutes until puffed and firm. Turn out onto plates and serve with crème fraîche.

Why choose organic?
Allowed to ripen on the tree and picked at maturity, organic apples will have a much higher vitamin content.
- 105 calories per 100 g
- Provides useful amounts of protein, fibre, selenium, iodine, vitamin B_{12}, folic acid, vitamins A, C and E
- Ellagic acid and pectin from the apples are, respectively, cancer-fighting and an excellent digestive aid

Organic gardener's tip
If you've got apple trees in your garden, plant a clump of garlic chives under each tree to protect against scab. They're also a wonderful cut-and-come-again plant for flavouring savoury dishes.

Don't dismiss prunes as being purely medicinal. As well as being highly nutritious and one of the richest sources of protective antioxidants, their distinctive flavour is delicate and memorable, especially when combined with the tang of lemon. The flavour of organic prunes more than justifies their cost.

perfect organic prune purée

Serves 4

stoned prunes	450 g (1 lb)
lemon juice	from 2, unwaxed
lemon zest	from 1, unwaxed
demerara sugar	45 g (1½ oz)
salt	1 small pinch
egg-whites	3 free-range

1 Place the prunes in a bowl, cover with boiling water and leave to soak overnight. Chop coarsely.

2 Place all the other ingredients in a bowl, and whisk till the mixture stiffens. Fold in prunes and refrigerate for two hours.

3 Serve with low-fat natural yoghurt containing zest of the other lemon and quarter of a teaspoon of allspice, if desired.

Why choose organic?

Non-organic prunes are often coated with mineral oil as well as being subject to fungicides, insecticides and pesticides, making them highly unsuitable during pregnancy.

• 136 calories per 100 g

• Provides lots of fibre and potassium, which helps control blood pressure, and good amounts of iron, selenium, and vitamin B_6

• Unfortunately, constipation is a common problem during pregnancy, so benefit from the gentle laxative effect of succulent organic prunes

menus for a healthy pregnancy

If you're pregnant or breastfeeding, there are two vital rules:

1 *Don't* try to keep your weight down, and never follow any low-calorie weight-loss diets unless advised to do so by your doctor;

2 However, don't use "I'm eating for two" as an excuse for pigging out on every bar of chocolate, piece of cake or sticky bun you can get your hands on – even if they are organic!

What you do need is a healthy, balanced diet of good, wholesome and – above all – organic foods. Yes, you must have an increased consumption of some essential nutrients; for instance, your protein intake should rise from around 45 grams a day to 51 during pregnancy and 56 during breastfeeding. You should double your folic acid content, have more vitamin C and a bit more vitamin A. I would also suggest that you take in more calcium, phosphorus, magnesium, zinc, copper and selenium, though the government advice is that you only need increased amounts while breastfeeding. These menus are a guide to compiling the best eating plan for you and your developing or nursing baby.

Light Lunch

Josceline's Ultimate Potato Salad (p 89)

1 slice World's Easiest Wholemeal Bread (p 106)

60 g (2 oz) any hard organic cheese

A ripe pear

Essential oils, fibre, B vitamins and lots of calcium to build strong bones for you and the baby make this an ideal lunch.

Light Supper

Free-range Spanish Omelette (p 58)

A watercress and green leaf salad

Tessa's Own Tomato and Olive Oil Dressing (p 87)

A banana with 1 small carton of natural low-fat live yoghurt

Protein and lecithin from the eggs, protective antioxidants, iron and vitamin C from the salad and potassium from the banana make a sustaining and nourishing combination for mothers and developing babies alike.

A Quick Healthy Snack

Randolph's Organic Rarebit (p 60)

Conserve your time and energy with this easy dish, which also provides protein, calcium and B vitamins

Summer Sunday Brunch
Beet-treat Soup (p 86)

Wild Mushroom and Radicchio Salad (p 88)

Cheese and Bread Pudding (p 61)

Being pregnant and and feeling tired are constant companions. Boost your energy levels with this delicious menu. It provides lots of good calories, huge quantities of beta-carotene and a hint of naughtiness in the pudding.

Lunch for Friends
Pasta Organic with Raw Courgette (p 90)

Wild Salmon Moutarde (p 92)

Runner beans

Steamed carrots

Perfect Organic Prune Purée (p 97)

Halfway through a pregnancy doesn't seem like the best time to be entertaining, but this quick and easy menu won't tax your strength – and it is sure to delight your companions.

A Dinner Party

French Onion Soup (p 85)

Joe's Organic Highgrove Beef (p 95)

New potatoes boiled in their skins

Spring greens

Villandry Organic Apple Flans (p 96)

This simple menu combines the antibacterial benefits of onions with the body-building nutrients of organic beef.

Chemical residues in foods pose a threat to adults, but think how much more harmful they can be to a developing infant. Your baby's central nervous system and immune system are immature, making it more vulnerable to damage from toxic residues. These, especially in the form of pesticides, are a growing cause for concern. In the US, for example, the American Environmental Working Group reports alarming evidence of organophosphate residues in commercial baby food. In the UK, government

organic food

statistics reveal that some British-made baby foods contain many times the safe level of pesticide residues allowed by EU law – and a significant percentage of them harbour more than one.

Some leading allergy experts believe that it isn't atmospheric pollution that causes asthma in children, but possible chemical damage to their immune systems. Add to this the huge list of artificial additives that find their way into various foods (*see* pp 14–15), and you'll see why it is vital to use as much organic produce as possible when feeding babies and children.

WHAT TO FEED AND WHEN All babies have their own time-scales, and you'll soon find what's right for your child. However, the following is a general guideline for feeding.

For the first four to six months of life, the best thing for your baby is its mother's breast milk. Between four and five months, you can introduce some puréed organic vegetables and fruits. Offering a spoon or two in the middle of a breast- or bottle-feed is a useful trick. In the early stages of weaning, restrict your recipes to two or a maximum of three ingredients, slowly increasing the number as your baby gets older. Introduce new foods gradually, not more than one every three or four days.

or babies

First weaning foods should be puréed and thinned with cooking water, cooled boiled water, or breast or organic formula milk.

Between approximately six to nine months, your baby will be ready for slightly lumpier dishes of mashed, minced or finger foods rather than purées. Start feeding rice, mashed potatoes, plain yoghurt, but avoid cow's milk, wheat-based products, eggs, nuts, nut butters and citrus fruits because of possible allergic reactions.

If your child shows obvious signs of allergy to any food, then omit it for a few weeks and try again. Take particular care if there is a history of allergies in either parent's family, but don't cut out any of the major food groups without professional advice. By 11 to 12 months, your baby should be ready for just about anything.

purées and first foods

In addition to the obvious health benefits, preparing your own organic baby food is the best way to ensure that your baby enjoys the full delights of food flavours. In spite of warnings against feeding herbs, spices, onions and garlic to babies, I've never found these to cause the slightest problem – except in the case of hot chillies. Discretion, however, is essential: you need only a sprinkle of parsley, a hint of onion, garlic, bay leaf, thyme, rosemary or any other herb. This makes it much easier when you feed your baby from the family meal: no one has to suffer blandness. Still, it's best to start slowly, using simple single purées such as the ones listed below. These minimise the risk of allergic reactions and appeal more easily to your baby's as yet undeveloped sense of taste.

Single Ingredient Purées
1 Wash, peel, core and chop an organic apple or pear, or shell a few organic peas.
2 Cook in a little boiling unsalted water until soft. Strain and keep the water, then purée, using the cooking water or plain boiled water, or breast or organic formula milk to thin as required.

Banana Purée
Bananas are an ideal early weaning food, supplying good calories, B vitamins and some vitamin C. Unfortunately, non-organic bananas are also one of the most sprayed crops: the majority of them contain traces of chemical residues. Most growers apply around 40 pounds a year of pesticides, herbicides and insecticides to every acre on their plantations – so organic bananas are a real must. Unripe bananas are indigestible for a baby's immature digestive system. Wait until the skins are starting to turn a speckled brown, then purée a small piece of banana and offer it on a spoon. Most babies take to them instantly.

Carrot and Apple Purée
1 Wash, peel, chop and core one organic apple. Wash, peel and chop one small organic carrot.
2 Bring to the boil in enough water to cover; simmer until thoroughly cooked (eight to ten minutes).
3 Strain, reserving the water. Purée and mix to a suitable consistency using reserved water, cooled boiled water, breast or organic formula milk.

Apple and Apricot Purée

1 Wash, peel, chop and core one organic apple, and wash and stone two fresh organic apricots.
2 Bring to the boil in enough water to cover; simmer until thoroughly cooked (eight to ten minutes).
3 Strain, reserving the water. Purée and mix to a suitable consistency using reserved water, cooled boiled water, breast or organic formula milk.

Lizzie Vann's Banana Porridge

No one has done as much to revolutionise the baby market in recent years as Lizzie Vann, founder of the Baby Organix baby-food company. This is her recipe for a treat most infants can't get enough of, and it's a wonderful source of energy, minerals and B vitamins. Note: for six- to seven-month-olds, use organic oats straight from the packet and add a spoonful of washed organic sultanas; for younger babies, grind the oats to a fine meal; a cleaned coffee grinder is perfect or alternatively you can use a mortar and pestle.

1 Put two dessertspoons of oats or finely ground oatmeal into a saucepan with five dessertspoons of water, breast or organic formula milk, or a mixture.
2 Bring gently to the boil, stirring only occasionally. Simmer gently until cooked, stirring in order to prevent sticking.
3 Mash half a ripe banana and mix with the porridge.

Swede, Parsnip and Potato Purée

1 Wash, peel and chop one small organic potato, a quarter of an organic swede and a small organic parsnip – approximately equal amounts of each.
2 Bring to the boil in enough water to cover; simmer gently until cooked (around ten minutes).
3 Strain, reserving the water. Purée and mix to a suitable consistency using reserved water, cooled boiled water, breast or organic formula milk.

Broccoli, Green Bean and Sweet Potato Purée

By five to six months, you can start to introduce some organic green vegetables.
1 Wash and chop a little broccoli, a few French or runner beans (remove any strings) and half a peeled sweet potato.
2 Put the chopped sweet potato in enough water to cover, bring to the boil and simmer. After five minutes, add the broccoli and beans.
3 Cook for another five or six minutes until vegetables are all soft. Strain, reserving the water.
4 Purée and mix to a suitable consistency using reserved water, cooled boiled water, breast or organic formula milk.

organic recipes for older babies

Organic Cheese, Spinach and Potato Purée (suitable for six-month-olds)

1 Wash, peel and chop a medium organic potato, place in enough water to cover, bring to the boil and simmer.

2 Thoroughly wash a small handful of fresh organic spinach, but don't dry. When the potato is nearly ready, put the spinach in a saucepan, cover and cook till soft.

3 Combine spinach, potato and one ounce of grated organic cheese and purée together.

Mix to a suitable consistency using reserved vegetable water, cooled boiled water, breast or organic formula milk.

Note: by seven months it's time to add pasta, beans, chickpeas, chicken, meat and fish. You should be able to abandon the purées and move on to slightly lumpier foods, as your baby will probably have enough teeth and the ability to chew. But first:

A Taste of Brussels Sprouts

This recipe provides beta-carotene, vitamin C, folic acid, a little fibre, plenty of minerals and most importantly, new tastes.

1 From your own meal, save two Brussels sprouts, two boiled potatoes and two carrots – all of which should be cooked without salt.

2 While they're still warm, put them through the coarse disk of your mouli.

Roast Chicken with Pumpkin, Peas and Sweetcorn

Protein, carbohydrate, lots of beta-carotene, B vitamins and a good selection of minerals abound in this quick and easy meal.

1 Make sure your organic chicken is completely cooked through by piercing the thickest part of the thigh with a skewer: juices must run clear, not pink. Cut off a small piece of breast without the skin and chop quite finely before putting through the coarse mouli disk with the vegetables.

2 Cook the pumpkin, peas and sweetcorn (organic frozen will do, but not tinned) in unsalted water. Reserve the vegetable water in case you need to thin the purée a little.

3 Purée all together in the mouli for a highly nutritious baby meal.

organic recipes for older children

Here are just a few recipe ideas for older children and teenagers, including some vegetarian recipes. These are tried and tested and most youngsters will enjoy them with relish – organic, of course!

organic lamb burgers

Serves 4

wholemeal bread	1 slice, without crusts
minced lamb	450 g (1 lb)
onion	1 large, grated or finely chopped
egg	1 medium, free-range
fresh oregano	1 pinch
fresh thyme	1 pinch
fresh parsley	1 tablespoon, chopped
fresh mint	1 tablespoon, chopped
salt	1 pinch
black pepper	freshly ground to taste

Most youngsters enjoy burgers, and these, made from organic lean lamb, are especially delicious. Served with crunchy iceberg lettuce, ripe tomatoes and a good wholemeal bun, it's a complete meal.

1 Soak the bread in water, then squeeze out the excess.

2 If you have a food processor, put in all the ingredients and process. Alternatively, mix by hand: crumble the bread into a bowl with the minced lamb, grated onion, beaten egg and seasoning.

3 Shape into four burgers, oil the grill rack and cook under a high grill for about four minutes each side.

Chef's tip

Buy your lamb when it's cheapest, mince it and freeze it in 450-g (1-lb) packs for later use.

Why choose organic?

Non-organic meat is a real worry since organochloride pesticides tend to be accumulated and stored in animal fat.

- 150 calories per 100 g
- Provides loads of protein, iron, zinc, vitamin B_{12}, and useful amounts of other minerals and B vitamins. This is a real blood- and body-building dish for growing youngsters, with less than 10% fat

Apart from feeding your children the organic way, you can also teach them how to cook, a skill that will prove an invaluable source of health and pleasure for the rest of their lives. Why not start with this homemade bread recipe? Most kids love getting their hands in the dough. I make variations of this wonderful loaf by mixing different flours: a half a pound of white, rye, or buckwheat to one pound of wholemeal. You can also add chopped walnuts, pumpkin seeds or poppy seeds.

world's easiest
wholemeal bread

wholemeal bread flour	680 g (1 lb 8oz), stoneground
easy-blend dried yeast	1 x 7 g sachet
salt	½ teaspoon
olive oil	2 teaspoons, extra virgin
molasses	1 teaspoon
lukewarm water	600 ml (20 fl oz)
sunflower seeds	2 dessertspoons (optional)
bread tin	1 x 900 g (2 lb), warm and lightly oiled

Why choose organic?

Massive application of synthetic fertilisers are applied to non-organic wheat, as well as herbicides, insecticides and fungicides, including persistent organophosphates and synthetic pyrethrums.

- 215 calories per 100 g
- Provides lots of fibre, protein and B vitamins

1 Preheat oven to 200°C (400°F/gas mark 6).

2 Mix together flour and yeast. Dissolve the salt, oil and molasses in the water.

3 Make a well in the flour and add the liquid and the sunflower seeds. Knead energetically for three to four minutes, or until the dough comes away without sticking to the sides of the bowl. (Add more flour if it's too sticky or water if dry and crumbly.)

4 Put the dough into the bread tin, cover with a clean, wet cloth and leave to rise in a warm place for 30 to 40 minutes, or until dough is near the top of the tin.

5 Bake in the middle of the oven for 35 to 40 minutes. Tap the bottom, if it sounds hollow, it's done; if not, bake for another five minutes. Cool on a wire rack.

stuffed
organic
peppers

Serves 4

red, yellow, or orange peppers	4 large
brown rice	175 g (6 oz), long-grain
water	400 ml (14 fl oz)
onion	1 medium, finely sliced
olive oil	1 tablespoon, extra virgin
pine nuts	1 tablespoon
seedless raisins	1 tablespoon
fresh mint	1 tablespoon, finely chopped
fresh parsley	1 tablespoon, chopped
sea salt	to taste
black pepper	freshly ground to taste
parmesan	4 tablespoons, grated

A great dish if you've got a vegetarian in the family. Peppers are a wonderful source of nutrients – particularly the highly protective carotenoids which are abundant in the red, yellow and orange varieties.

1 Preheat oven to 190°C (375°F/gas mark 5). Wash peppers, remove the top with the stalk but do not discard, and scoop out the ribs and the seeds.

2 Wash the rice. Bring the water to the boil; add the rice, cover and cook until done, approximately 30 to 40 minutes. Leave uncovered in the pan to dry.

3 In a frying pan, gently sweat the onions in the olive oil, but don't brown. Add the pine nuts and raisins and sauté for a few moments.

4 Mix the onions, raisins and fresh herbs with the rice, season with salt and pepper and fill the peppers with the mixture, leaving a one centimetre (half-inch) gap at the top.

5 Wedge peppers into an ovenproof dish small enough to keep them upright, add boiling water until they are half covered, replace the tops and drizzle with a little olive oil. Cover with foil, and cook in the oven for 40 minutes.

6 Pour off any remaining water. Remove lids from the peppers and fill the top of each with grated cheese.
Put under a hot grill until bubbling and just turning brown. They're delicious hot or cold.

Why choose organic?

The great bonus of organic peppers is that they are not the tasteless water-filled products of hydroponics, but are delicious and nutrient-dense.

- 200 calories per 100 g
- Provides lots of protein, calcium, folic acid, vitamins A, C and E, and protective antioxidants
- A perfect immune-boosting dish for youngsters of any age

quick organic spinach snack

Serves 4

garlic	2 cloves
olive oil	4 tablespoons, extra virgin
pine nuts	1 small handful
baby spinach	500 g (1 lb 2 oz)
wholemeal bread	2 thick slices
lemon	juice of 1 medium

It's not always easy to get children to eat spinach, but cook it like this and serve it like the Italians – warm rather than hot – and you'll be surprised how much they enjoy it. This is a simple, quick, full-of-goodness recipe for two hungry youngsters.

1 Slice the garlic and sweat gently in the oil for five minutes, without browning. Add the pine nuts and cook for another five minutes.
2 Wash the spinach, put in a large saucepan with no extra water and cook covered until thoroughly wilted. Leave to cool.
3 Add the warm oil, garlic, pine nuts and the lemon juice. Stir well and arrange on the bread.

Why choose organic?

Non-organic spinach frequently contains high levels of nitrates

• 142 calories per 100 g

• Provides lots of protein, hardly any saturated fat, plenty of fibre, calcium, potassium, iron, zinc, and huge amounts of folic acid, vitamins A and E

• Spinach also supplies very special carotenoids which are essential for healthy eyes

bread and tomato salad

Serves 4

olive oil	3 tablespoons, extra virgin
garlic	2 cloves
bread	4 thick slices, without crusts , cut into cubes
tomatoes	6, ripe, plum
lemon juice	1 tablespoon
sea salt	to taste
black pepper	freshly ground to taste
fresh basil	2 tablespoons, torn

Just bursting with Mediterranean sunshine, this salad uses ripe, organic plum tomatoes when they're at their best and most flavour-packed. It works only with coarse, homemade organic wholemeal bread or good organic country bread.

1 Heat the oil in a large, deep frying pan. Chop the garlic and add with the bread to the oil. Stir continuously until the bread becomes crispy.

2 Wash and roughly chop the tomatoes. Put the bread cubes into a bowl, add the tomatoes, lemon juice, plenty of freshly milled black pepper, a pinch of sea salt and the basil. Toss well.

Why choose organic?

Chemical residues have been found in more than half the non-organic UK-produced tomatoes and in 60% of non-organic imported crops.

• 138 calories per 100 g

• Provides useful amounts of protein, virtually no saturated fat, lots of potassium, folic acid, vitamins C and E, and useful amounts of vitamin A, niacin, and selenium

• Rich in heart-protective and cancer-fighting lycopene from the tomatoes

dove's farm
scones

When Clare Marriage of Dove's Farm Foods, makers of organic flours, gave me this recipe, it brought back wonderful memories of cricket-club teas. Making these scones with oil instead of butter means you don't have to feel guilty about the whipped cream.

Self-raising flour	225 g (8 oz)
baking powder	2 level teaspoons
demerara sugar	1 tablespoon
olive oil	2 tablespoons, extra virgin
semi-skimmed milk	to mix
To finish:	homemade or organic jam, whipped cream

1 Preheat oven to 220°C (425°F/gas mark 7).

2 Mix together the flour, baking powder and sugar. Stir in the oil, then enough milk to form a soft ball of dough.

3 Turn out the dough onto a floured surface and flatten with your hands until 2 cm (¾ in) thick. Using a small cup or pastry cutter, press out circles of dough and place them on a floured baking tray. Bake for eight to ten minutes.

4 Cool on a wire rack, then split, spread with jam and whipped cream.

Why choose organic?

Non-organic cereal grains are often exposed to massive applications of synthetic fertilisers.

• At just under 40 calories each (without jam and cream), these are not just a taste treat but a useful contribution to your child's nutrition

spiced organic
apricots

This is an excellent, healthy and tasty dessert to keep in the fridge for the frequent snack-attacks that children get. When available, you can use fresh organic apricots.

dried apricots	225 g (8 oz)
cloves	4 whole
apple juice	400 ml (14 oz)
allspice	½ teaspoon
grated orange peel	from 1, unwaxed
cinnamon stick	1 small
runny honey	1 tablespoon
ground nutmeg	½ teaspoon

1 Wash the apricots thoroughly, then place in a pan with the apple juice, spices, orange peel, and honey. Bring to the boil.

2 Turn down the heat, and simmer over a very low heat until the apricots are tender.

3 Add extra calcium and beneficial bacteria by serving with organic live yoghurt.

Why choose organic?

When using dried fruits it's almost more important to choose organic as non-organic varieties are not only subjected to chemicals when they're growing, but are also treated after drying with antifungals and oils.

• 98 calories per 100 g

• Provides a little protein, no fat, and lots of fibre

• Apricots are an enormous source of potassium, and this dish also contains valuable amounts of vitamins A and C or

buying
ganic

guarantees and certification

The term "organic" is strictly defined by law, but to be certain that the food you are buying is genuinely organic, check that the label carries one of the recognised organic symbols. By far the most widespread approved mark in the UK is that of The Soil Association, which covers around 70 per cent of all certified organic food on sale in Britain. However, there are five other registering bodies that also guarantee the organic nature of goods. Listed below, they apply stringent rules and regular inspections to ensure the truly organic nature of all food, drink and other products which bear their symbols.

 The Soil Association, Bristol House, 40–56 Victoria Street, Bristol BS1 6BY. Tel: 0117 929 0661

 The Biodynamic Agricultural Association, Painswick Inn Project, Gloucester Street, Stroud, Gloucestershire GL5 1QG. Tel: 01453 759501

 The Irish Organic Farmers and Growers Association, Harbour Building, Harbour Road, Kilbeggan, County Westmeath. Tel: 0506 32563

 Organic Farmers and Growers, Views Farm, Great Milton, Oxford, Oxfordshire, OX9 7NW. Tel: 01844 279352

 The Scottish Organic Producers Association, Milton of Cambus, Doone, Perthshire FK16 6HG. Tel: 01786 841657

 UKROFS, the UK Register of Organic Food Standards, Ministry of Agriculture, Fisheries and Food, Nobel House, 17 Smith Square, London SW1P 3JR. Tel: 0171 238 5915

Strict rules also apply to the way in which farm animals are fed, kept and reared. Animal welfare is the first requirement, and for their by-products to be organic, the animals' food must be organic, too. It goes without saying that the use of routine antibiotics in feed, and hormones to promote growth or milk production are forbidden. If organic products are imported, then EU regulations demand that they are certified to the same standards as those applied in the UK and the rest of the EU. Unfortunately, a large proportion of organic goods do come from abroad, as there is still insufficient production in the UK to meet the growing demand. Sales of organic food have soared, and though the major supermarket chains have made a concerted effort to carry more organic produce, demand continues to exceed supply. Tesco alone reports that sales of organic foods have risen by 100 per cent in just one year. Sainsbury's is selling more than £1 million of organic products every week. Waitrose, which sells more than 600 organic products, reports that organic vegetables represent 8.5 per cent, dairy products ten per cent and baby foods 40 per cent of its total organic sales.

Through an American subsidiary, Sainsbury's already owns four completely organic supermarkets, and with luck, it won't be long before we see this type of operation in Britain. While you can already shop in a number of "organic-only" supermarkets, the majority of organic produce is purchased through farm shops, health-food stores, specialist food shops and through the hugely successful box-delivery schemes set up by The Soil Association.

There is no doubt that most organic produce demands a premium. Although farmers save money by not using expensive agrochemicals and synthetic fertilisers, the yields are smaller and production much more labour intensive. A major problem for growers is the length of time it takes to convert from non-organic to certified organic, and during this period farmers are incurring extra costs for no extra return. Government subsidies are minimal for organic farmers compared to the huge amounts paid to non-organic farmers for not growing crops, for guaranteed prices and in the form of EU hand-outs.

At least one supermarket, Waitrose, is addressing this problem by selling products from farms in the process of conversion as "transitional products". While these products are not certified organic – it takes several years for chemical residues to be leached out of the soil – crops and livestock are reared without the use of pesticides, insecticides, antibiotics and hormones. Farmers receive a small premium price for these goods and they are sold in the supermarket at prices which fall somewhere between non-organic and organic.

If you use a box scheme for your organic foods, you'll be pleasantly surprised by some prices. Since these schemes are often run by local farmers supplying you with seasonal produce, the costs will often be below those of your local supermarket's non-organic goods.

In the long run, of course, you can't measure health in terms of cost. Spending a little extra on organic food means less sickness and disease, less time off school for your children, and less time off work for adults. It increases the chances of a long, active and healthy retirement for the older members of society. It improves the quality of the environment we all live in and reduces the risks of polluting our planet beyond the point of no return.

Without question, going organic will be the best investment you can possibly make in terms of huge returns on minimal expenditure.

directory of shops and suppliers

Happily, it's now becoming relatively easy to buy organic food. Most supermarkets stock some organic lines, but they ought to be stocking more. There are also thousands of health shops, farm shops, box-scheme retailers and mail-order companies selling organic food, and restaurants which use only organic items in the dishes on their menus. There are far too many to include them all, but here are some that I've tracked down throughout the country.

ENGLAND

NORTHEAST

Brunswick Organic Nursery, Appleton Rd, Bishopthorpe, York YO23 2RF. Tel: 01904 701869. Farm-grown vegetables, apples, plums, 100 varieties of herbs, plus organic cottage garden plants. *Farm shop.*

Down To Earth, 406 Sharrowvale Rd, Hunters Bar, Sheffield S11 8ZP. Tel: 0114 268 5220. General vegetarian wholefoods in stock. Can order any vegetarian organic produce, including clothing made from organic fibres. *Shop.*

The Green Shop, 54 Bridge St, Berwick upon Tweed, Northumberland TD15 1AQ. Tel: 01289 330897. Fruit, vegetables, eggs, dairy produce, general wholefoods, herbs, organic clothing and bedding, and a wide range of organic alcoholic drinks, including wine, beer, cider, Champagne, saki and sherry. *Shop.*

HDRA Organic Wine Club, 261 Upper Town St, Bramley, Leeds LS13 3JT. Tel: 0113 257 7545. Wine, beer, cider, juices and organic Calvados. *Mail order, restaurants and wholesale, by the case.*

Nature's Trail, 665 Ecclesall Rd, Hunters Bar, Sheffield, S11 8PT. Tel: 0114 266 5984. Soya milk and yoghurt, vegetable juices and general wholefoods. *Shop, nationwide mail order for a range of food supplements.*

Out of this World, Gosforth Shopping Centre, High St, Newcastle-upon-Tyne NE3 1JZ. Tel: 0191 213 0421. Wine, beer, cider, bread, fruit, vegetables, herbs, eggs, dairy produce, beef, pork, bacon, lamb, poultry, general wholefoods and baby foods. *Shop, nationwide mail order.*

Simply Organic, Sandylands, Market Weighton Rd, Barlby, Selby, N. Yorks YO8 7LB. Tel: 01757 708540. Chicken, lamb, beef, pork, bread, fruit, vegetables, eggs, dairy produce, wholefoods and herbs. *Shop.*

Your Nuts, Springfield Mill, Norman Road, Denby Dale, Huddersfield HD8 8TH. Tel: 01484 864902. *And at* 14a Towngate, Holmfirth, Kirklees HD7 1HA. Tel: 01484 680126. Local bread and general wholefoods. *Shop.*

NORTHWEST

Chorlton Wholefoods, 34 Beech Road, Chorlton-Cum-Hardy, Trafford M21 9EL. Tel: 0161 881 6399.
Bread, fruit, vegetables, herbs, eggs, dairy produce and general wholefoods. *Shop, home deliveries.*

Demeter Wholefoods, 12 Welles St, Sandbach, Cheshire CW11 1GT. Tel: 01270 760445.
Wine, bread, fruit, vegetables, dairy produce and general wholefoods. *Shop, nationwide mail order.*

Kan Foods, 9 New Shambles, Kendal, Cumbria LA9 4TS. Tel: 01539 721190.
Fruit, vegetables, herbs, dairy produce and general wholefoods. *Shop, mail order (dried goods only).*

Mossley Wholefoods, 11 & 13 Arundle St, Mossley, Tameside OL5 ONY. Tel: 01457 837743.
Wine, fruit, vegetables, dairy produce and general wholefoods. *Shop, free delivery within 10 miles.*

The Village Bakery and Restaurant, Melmerby, Penrith, Cumbria, CA10 1HE. Tel: 01768 881515.
Bread, pastries, pies, puddings, baking supplies. *Shop, nationwide mail order.*

EAST

Camphill Communities East Anglia,
Thornage Hall, Holt, Norfolk NR25 7QH.
Tel: 01263 860305.
Vegetables, meat, herbs and cereals. *Phone to order and collect from Thornage Hall.*

Loaves and Fishes, 52 Thoroughfare, Woodbridge, Suffolk IP12 1AL. Tel: 012394 385650.
Wine, bread, fruit, vegetables, meat, dairy, wholefoods, herbs and natural remedies. *Shop.*

Maud Foster Mill, Willoughby Rd, Boston, Lincolnshire PE21 9EG. Tel: 01205 352188.
15 varieties of flour stone-ground on the premises. *Shop and windmill.*

Naturally Yours, The Horse and Gate Farm, Whitcham Toll, Ely, Cambs CB6 2AB. Tel: 01353 778723.
Meat, vegetable boxes, cheese, fruit, flour and general wholefoods. *Shop, box scheme, home deliveries within 50 miles.*

Organic Connections International, Riverdale, Town Rd, Upwell, Wisbech, Cambs PE14 9AF.
Tel: 01945 773374.
Salads, fruit, pasta, eggs, wholefoods, herbs and wine. *Box scheme, local home deliveries.*

Pure Suffolk Foods Ltd, Unit 5c, Eastlands Industrial Estate, Leiston, Suffolk IP16 4LL. Tel: 01728 830575.
Meat and poultry. *Mail order, free delivery in Suffolk, courier for elsewhere.*

MIDLANDS

Good Food Shop, 475–477 Hartshill Road, Hartshill, Stoke-on-Trent, Staffordshire ST4 6AA.
Tel: 01782 710234.
Meat, poultry, fish, frozen vegetables and organic cheese. *Shop, box scheme, nationwide delivery.*

Growing Concern, Home Farm, Woodhouse Lane, Nanpanton, Loughborough, Leicestershire, LE11 3YG.
Tel: 01509 239228.
Rare-breed meat, including Hereford beef, smoked produce, bread, game, poultry, cheese, sausages, eggs, fruit and vegetables. *Farm shop.*

Market Wholefoods, The Shambles, 1a Mellor Rd,
New Mills, High Peak, via Stockport, Derbyshire
SK12 4DW. Tel: 01663 747550.
Wine, bread, fruit, vegetables, meat, eggs, dairy and
general wholefoods. *Shop, box scheme, home delivery
within 30 miles.*

Organic Health, 23 Market St, Heanor, Derbyshire
DE75 7NR. Tel: 01773 717718.
Wine, bread, fruit, vegetables, herbs meat, eggs, dairy
and general wholefoods. *Shop, mail order.*

Oat Cuisine, 47 Broad St, Ross-on-Wye, Herefordshire
HR9 7DY. Tel: 01989 566271.
Bread, eggs, dairy produce and general wholefoods.
Shop, bistro, take-away.

Organic Enterprises, Henry Doubleday Research
Association, Ryton Organic Gardens, Coventry CV8 3LG.
Tel: 01203 308201.
Beef, pork, lamb, poultry, wine, bread, fruit, vegetables,
herbs, eggs, dairy produce and general wholefoods.
Shop, box scheme, restaurant.

Organic Roots, Crabtree Farm, Dark Lane,
King's Norton, Birmingham B23 0BS.
Tel: 01564 822294.
Bread, home-grown fruit and vegetables, herbs, fish,
meat, eggs, dairy and general wholefoods. *Farm shop.*

Prospect Organic Growers' Farm Shop,
Prospect Cottage, Bartestree, Hereford HR1 4BY.
Tel: 01432 851164.
Chicken, beef, pork, mutton, lamb, venison, bread,
home-grown fruit and vegetables, cheese, eggs, dairy
produce and general wholefoods. *Farm shop.*

HOME COUNTIES

Ash Green Organic Foods, Brickhurst Farm,
Hastings Rd, Pembury, Kent. Tel: 01892 838070.
Bread, fruit, vegetables, meat, dairy produce and
general wholefoods. *Farm shop, market stall,
home delivery.*

Cook's Delight, 360–4 High St, Berkhamsted.
Hertfordshire HP4 1HU. Tel: 01442 863584.
Can supply everything organic. *Shop, mail order*

Dove's Farm Foods Ltd, Salisbury Rd, Hungerford,
Berkshire RG17 0RF. Tel: 01488 684880.
Flour, biscuits and breakfast cereals. *Farm shop,
mail order.*

Eastwoods of Berkhamsted, 15 Gravel Path,
Berkhamsted, Hertfordshire HP4 2EF. Tel: 01442 865012.
Meat, including beef from Highgrove, poultry, cheese,
fruit, herbs, juices and biscuits.*Shop, mail order.*

The Fat Duck Restaurant, High St, Bray, Berkshire SL6
2AQ. Tel: 01628 580333.
Chef/proprietor Heston Blumenthal is a self-taught and
innovative creator of wonderful food. While not certified
100% organic, it's as organic as he can possibly make it,
especially his free-range meat and poultry. *Restaurant.*

Fieldfare Organics, Oakcroft, Dudswell Lane,
Berkhamsted, Hertfordshire HP4 3TQ. Tel: 01442 877363.
Fruit, vegetables, eggs and dairy produce.
Home deliveries.

Kulika Charitable Trust, Warren Farm, Rectory Rd,
Streatley, Berkshire RG8 9QE. Tel: 01491 872149.
Meat, eggs, vegetables and general wholefoods.
Farm shop, local home deliveries.

Nature's Harvest, 19 North St, Leighton Buzzard, Bedfordshire LU7 7EF. Tel: 01525 371378.
Flour, wheat, non-dairy alternatives and general wholefoods. *Shop.*

The Organic Beef Company, The Swan Inn, Inkpen, Hungerford, Berkshire RG17 9DX. Tel: 01488 668429.
Meat, wine, dried goods. *Farm shop, home deliveries.*

The Pumpkin Patch, 10 High St, Banstead, Surrey SM7 2LJ. Tel: 01737 371007.
Bread, fruit, eggs, dairy products, dried goods, herbs and supplements. *Shop.*

Yalding Organic Gardens, Benover Rd, Yalding, nr Maidstone, Kent MEJ 6EX. Tel: 01622 814650.
Dry foods. *Shop.*

LONDON

Bistrorganics, 46 Golborne Road, London W10 5PR.
Reservations tel: 0181 968 2200.
Leading chef Antony Worrell Thompson, like many chefs, is a great fan of organic food. He now has a five-acre organic smallholding from which he supplies this, his newest venture. When chefs of his calibre turn organic, you can expect culinary delights that show how far organic food has come from the kaftan, brown rice and sandals image of the Sixties. *Restaurant.*

Freshlands Health Store, 49 Parkway, Camden Town, London NW1 7PN. Tel: 0171 428 7575. *And at* 196 Old St, London EC1 9FR. Tel: 0171 250 1708.
Wine, bread, fruit, vegetables, herbs, eggs, dairy produce and general wholefoods. *Shops, with a salad and delicatessen bar at Camden Town.*

Joy, 511 Finchley Road, London NW3 7BB.
Tel: 0171 794 9308.
100% organic food shop, bread, cheese, oils, olives, nuts, homemade cakes, pastries, *charcuterie* and prepared food to take away. Organic outside catering, vegetarian or meat, dinner parties or banquets. *Shop.*

Joy at Aveda, 62–64 Weymouth Street, London W1 5PT.
Tel: 0171 487 5683.
Restaurant open during *shop* hours for organic food and good selection of organic breads and produce. Aveda at above address supplies amazing natural and organic cosmetics, skin care and beauty products.

Organics Direct Ltd, 1–7 Willow St, London EC2A 4BH.
Tel: 0171 729 2828.
Fruit and vegetables, dairy produce, milk, cheese, oils, bread, soup, cakes, herbs, crisps, baby food, fruit juices, wines and beers. *Mail order.*

Pharmacia, 169 Drury Lane, London WC2B 5QA.
Tel: 0171 831 0830.
Pharmacia offers a holistic approach to health care including "Liquid Health Solutions": organic fruit and vegetable juices with added herb extracts designed to increase your energy, brain power and immunity. *Shop*

Planet Organic, 42 Westbourne Grove, London W2 5SH.
Tel: 0171 221 7171.
Wine, bread, fruit, vegetables, herbs, meat, eggs, dairy produce and general wholefoods. *Shop, home deliveries.*

The Realfood Store, 14 Clifton Rd, Little Venice, London W9 1SS. Tel: 0171 266 1162.
Bread, fruit, vegetables, herbs, meat, eggs, dairy produce and general wholefoods. *Shop, home deliveries.*

Sauce barorganic diner, 214 Camden High St, London NW1 8QR. Tel: 0171 482 0777.
All-day restaurant/snack bar.

The Tea and Coffee Plant, 170 Portobello Rd, London W11 2EB. Tel: 0171 221 8137.
Tea, coffee, cocoa powder and herbal teas.*Shop, mail order.*

Villandry, 170 Great Portland St, London W1N 5TB. Tel: 0171 631 3131.
Wine, beer, fruit, vegetables, dairy produce, eggs, cheese, biscuits, meat, poultry, bottled goods, oils, vinegars, jams and chocolates. *Shop, restaurant.*

Wholefoods Ltd, 24 Paddington St, London W1M 4DR. Tel: 0171 935 3924.
London's first organic food shop with a wide range of vegetables, dairy products, eggs and bread. Also stocks supplements and health and organic gardening books. *Shop.*

Wild Oats, 210 Westbourne Grove, London W11 2RH. Tel: 0171 229 1063.
Stocks a wide range of organic foods, natural remedies and vitamins. *Shop.*

SOUTH

Boathouse Farm Shop, Boathouse Organic Farm, Isfield, Uckfield, East Sussex. Tel: 01825 750302.
Meat, poultry, eggs, vegetables and homemade produce. *Farm shop.*

Godshill Organics, Newport Rd, Godshill, Isle of Wight PQ38 3LY. Tel: 01983 840723.
Wine, fruit, vegetables, home-grown salads, herbs, eggs, dairy produce. *Shop, box scheme (June to January).*

Park Farm Shop, Park Farm, Heckfield, Hampshire RG27 0LD. Tel: 01189 326650.
Beef, pork, lamb, chicken, vegetables, fruit, dairy produce, flour and cereals. *Farm shop.*

Plaw Hatch Farm Ltd, Sharpthorne, East Grinstead, West Sussex RH19 4JL. Tel: 01342 810652.
Bacon, yoghurt, milk, cheese, cream, bread, fruit, eggs and general wholefoods. *Farm shop.*

Scragoak Farm,

Wine, sausages, bread, fruit, vegetables, herbs, eggs, dairy produce and general wholefoods.
Farm shop, box scheme (10% discount for members of The Soil Association).

Seasons Forest Row Ltd, 10 Hartfield Rd, Forest Row, East Sussex RH18 5DN. Tel: 01342 824673.
Bread, fruit, vegetables, herbs, meat, eggs, dairy produce and general wholefoods. *Shop, mail order to UK mainland.*

WEST

Eastbrook Farm, Bishopstone, Swindon, Wiltshire SN6 7PW. Tel: 01793 782211.
Mutton, veal, beef, poultry, home-cured ham and bacon, sausages and eggs. *Farm shop, mail order, home deliveries.*

Harvest Natural Foods, 224 Cheltenham Rd, Bristol BS6 5QU. Tel: 0117 9425997.
Bread, fruit, vegetables, eggs, dairy produce, chocolate, ice-cream and general wholefoods. *Shop, mail order.*

Hobbs House Bakery, 39 High St, Chipping Sodbury, Gloucestershire BS37 6BA. Tel: 01454 321629. *And at* 2 North Parade, Yate, Gloucestershire BS37 6AH. Bread and pastries. *Shop, mail order.*

Jekka's Herb Farm, Rose Cottage, Shellard's Lane, Alveston, Bristol BS35 3SY. Tel: 01454 418878. Jekka McVicar is the leading expert on growing, cultivating and using fresh herbs. Hundreds of different varieties are available, together with seeds and wildflowers. *Mail order.*

Living Earth Produce, Ruskin Mill, Old Bristol Rd, Nailsworth, Gloucestershire GL6 0LA. Tel: 01453 837510. Goat's milk and yoghurt, ice-cream, frozen meat, milk, cheese, bread, fruit, vegetable, herbs, eggs and general wholefoods. *Shop.*

The Organic Shop, The Square, Stow-on-the-Wold, Gloucestershire, GL54 1AB. Tel: 01451 831004. Wines, dairy produce, breads, meat and vegetables. *Shop, mail order, take-away.*

Pimhill Farm, Lea Hall, Harmer Hill, Shrewsbury, Shropshire SY4 3DY. Tel: 01939 290342. Over 2,000 organic lines including cheeses, dried goods, wines, vegetables and meats. *Shop, registered organic café serving all home-cooked foods.*

T & P Murray Ltd, 153 Gloucester Rd, Bishopston, Bristol BS7 8BA. Tel: 0117 942 4025. Beef, lamb and cheese, including freezer packs. *Shop, home deliveries, mail order*

Sunshine Health Shop, 25 Church St, Stroud, Gloucestershire GL5 1JL. Tel: 01453 763923. Homemade cakes and savouries, bread, fruit, vegetables, dairy produce and general wholefoods. *Shop, mail order.*

SOUTHWEST

Good Nature, 2 Esplanade, Fowey, Cornwall PL23 1HY. Tel: 01726 832110. Vegetables, herbs, bread, fruit, dairy produce, non-dairy alternatives, gluten-free produce and general wholefoods. *Shop, box scheme.*

Hambledon Herbs, Court Farm, Milverton, Somerset TA4 1NF. Tel: 01823 401205. More than 450 herbs and spices, herb teas, Christmas specialities. *Mail order.*

Higher Hacknell Farm, Burrington, Umberleigh, Devon EX37 9LX. Tel: 01769 560292. Fresh and frozen local beef and lamb, potatoes. *Farm shop, farm gate, box scheme, mail order.*

Little Ash Eco Farm, Throwleigh, Okehampton, Devon EX20 2QJ. Tel: 01647 231394. Oats, flour, wool, jam, vegetables, meat and dairy produce. *Farm shop.*

Roscombe Farm, 123 Union Street, Castle Circus, Torquay, Devon TQ1 3DW. Tel: 01803 293996. Ice-cream. *Shop, mail order.*

Stoneybridge Farm Shop, Stoneybridge Organic Nursey, Tywardreath, Par, Cornwall PL24 2TY. Tel: 01726 813858. Beef, chicken, lamb, pork, cheese, wine, fruit juice, beer, fruit, vegetables and herbs. *Farm shop.*

Swaddles Green Farm, Hare Lane, Buckland St Mary, Chard, Somerset TA20 3JR. Tel: 01460 234387. Meat, poultry, beer, wine, cheese. *Farm gate, home deliveries, mail order.*

Tregannic Farm, Drakewalls, Gunnislake, Cornwall
PL18 9ED. Tel: 01822 833969.
Vegetable boxes, fruit, lamb and eggs to order.
Box scheme, home deliveries.

West Country Organic Foods Ltd, Natson Farm,
Tedburn St Mary, Exeter, Devon EX6 6ET. Tel: 01647 24724.
Beef, lamb, pork, poultry, bacon, general wholefoods
and grocery, Christmas specialities. *Mail order.*

IRELAND

The Organic Food Market, Meeting House Square
Temple Bar, Dublin
Cheeses, meat, sausages, bread, fresh produce and
wonderful deli stall. *Open 8am every Saturday.*

Sheridan's Cheesemongers, Seamus Sheridan
11 South Anne St, Dublin 2. Tel: 01679 3143. *And at*
Kirwans Lane, Galway. Tel: 091 564 829.
A staggering selection of 100% farmhouse, handmade
Irish cheese together with other European cheeses,
many of them organic. *Shop.*

NORTHERN IRELAND

Ballylagan Organic Farm, 12 Ballylagan Rd, Straid,
Ballyclare BT39 9NF. Tel: 01960 322867.
Lamb and Aberdeen Angus beef in freezer packs,
home-grown vegetables. *Farm shop.*

Eat Well, 413 Lisburn Rd, Belfast BT9 7EW.
Tel: 01232 664362.
Bread, pulses, cereals, salads, herbs and general
wholefoods. *Shop, mail order, home deliveries.*

John McCormick, 13 Seaview Terrace, Holywood,
N Down. Tel: 01232 423063.
Fruit, vegetables, meat. *Farm shop, box scheme.*

Natural Foods, 19 Strand Rd, Derry. Tel: 01504 262939.
Home-grown vegetables. *Shop.*

SCOTLAND

L and M Allison, Sawmill Croft, Forglen, Turriff,
Aberdeenshire AB5 4JY. Tel: 01888 568501.
Vegetables. *Box scheme, deliveries to local distribution
points.*

Bellfield Organic Nursery, Strathmiglo, Fife KY14 7RH.
Tel: 01337 860764.
Fruit, vegetables and dried wholefoods. *Box scheme,
deliveries within roughly 50 miles.*

Evergreen Wholefoods, 18 Nithsdale Rd,
Pollockshields, Glasgow G41 2AN. Tel: 0141 422 1303.
Bread, ice-cream, fruit, vegetable, eggs and general
wholefoods. *Shop.*

Highland Harvest, 3 Cairnleith Croft, Ythanbank,
Ellon, Aberdeenshire AB41 7UB. Tel: 01358 761298.
Vegetables, potted herbs and seaweed meal (for
gardens and as a food supplement for cattle, sheep
and horses). *Farm shop, weekly home deliveries within
20 miles of Aberdeen.*

Highland Wholefoods, Unit 6, 13 Harbour Rd,
Longman Estate, Inverness IV1 1SY. Tel: 01463 712393.
Wine, bread, fruit, vegetables, herbs, eggs, dairy
produce and general wholefoods. *Shop, regular
deliveries to distribution points in Highland and
Grampian, and the islands.*

Loch Arthur Creamery, Beeswing, Dumfries, Dumfries and Galloway DG2 8JG. Tel: 01387 760296. Farm-made hard and soft cheeses, cream cheese, yoghurt, bread. Beef, lamb and pork for bulk orders. *Farm shop, nationwide mail order.*

Millstone Wholefoods, 15 High St, Oban, Argyll PA34 4BG. Tel: 01631 562704.
Bread, fruit, vegetables, eggs, dairy produce and general wholefoods and health-store produce. *Shop, mail order for herbal remedies, vitamins and essential oils, carrier service to the islands.*

The Organic Food Shop, 45 Broughton St, Edinburgh, EH1 3JU. Tel: 0131 556 1772.
2,000 organic lines, including fruit, vegetable, meat, cheese, dairy produce, wine, teas and vinegar. *Shop, home deliveries in central Edinburgh, nationwide box scheme.*

Organic Meat and Products LTD, Jamesfield Farm, Newburgh, Fife KY14 6EW. Tel: 01738 850498.
Beef, lamb, mutton, venison, bacon, sausages, haggis and vegetables. *Farm shop, nationwide mail order (except for vegetables).*

WALES

Country Kitchen, 10 Sea View Rd, Colwyn Bay, Conwy LL29 8DG. Tel: 01492 533329.
Bread, fruit, vegetables, dairy produce, general wholefoods. *Shop, mail order.*

Graig Farm, Dolau, Llandrindod Wells, Powys LD1 5TL. Tel: 01597 851655.
Beef, lamb, pork, mutton, chicken, herbs, homemade pies, dairy produce, general wholefoods. *Farm shop, mail order.*

Bob and Dot James, Rogerswell, Whitland, Pembrokeshire SA34 0QY. Tel: 01994 240237. Fruit, vegetables, meat and dairy produce. *Call and collect, home deliveries, box scheme.*

Whitebrook Organic Growers, The Old Rectory, Llanvaches, Newport NP6 3AY. Tel: 01633 400406. Fruit, vegetables, salads, squashes, fruit juice, cheese, dried goods. *Box scheme, home delivery.*

Wye Valley Plants, The Nortons, Tintern, Gwent NP6 7NX. Tel: 01291 689253.
More than 400 culinary and medicinal herbs. *Shop.*

WHOLESALE OUTLETS

Greencity Wholefoods, 23 Fleming St, Dennistoun, Glasgow G31 1PQ. Tel: 0141 554 7633.
Supplies dried wholefoods to cooperatives from the Borders to Aberdeen. *Minimum order: £150.*

useful addresses

The Soil Association,
Bristol House, 40–56 Victoria Street,
Bristol BS1 6BY. Tel: 0117 929 0661.

Action & Information on Sugars,
PO Box 459, London SE5 7QA.

The Banana Link, 38–40 Exchange
Street, Norwich, Norfolk NR2 1AX.
Tel: 01603 761 645.

Compassion in World Farming,
5 Charles Street, Petersfield, Hants
GU32 3EH. Tel: 01730 264 208.

Environment and Health News,
PO Box 1954, Somerset BA6 9FE.

The Food Commission,
94 White Lion Street, London N1 9PF.
Tel: 0171 837 2250.

Friends of the Earth,
26 Underwood Street, London
N1 7JT. Tel: 0171 490 1555.

Foresight, 28 The Paddock,
Godalming, Surrey GU7 1XD.
Tel: 01483 427 839.

Greenpeace UK,
Canonbury Villas, London N1 2PN.
Tel: 0171 865 8100.

**Henry Doubleday Research
Association (HDRA),**
Ryton Organic Gardens, Ryton-on-
Dunsmore, Coventry CV8 3LG.
Tel: 01203 303 517.

**Hyperactive Children's Support
Group,** 71 Whyke Lane, Chichester,
Sussex PO19 2LD. Tel: 01903 725182.

**Sustain Food and Farming
Alliance,** 94 White Lion Street,
London N1 9PF. Tel: 0171 837 1228.

The Pesticides Trust, Eurolink
Business Centre, 49 Effra Road,
London SW2 1BZ. Tel: 0171 274 8895.

appendices

Artificial sweeteners Artificial sweeteners are among the most over-used and under-publicised additives. They crop up almost everywhere – not just in low-calorie products. They may be found in many supposedly "ordinary" foods, including crisps, sweets, sauces, savoury dishes and even medicines, and we are constantly being told that they are perfectly safe.

Why, then, should Dr Michael Jacobson, director of Washington DC's Centre for Science in the Public Interest (CSPI), have serious reservations about the safety of these sweeteners? Well, there is saccharin, for one thing. Regarded as safe by the British government, saccharin has been used for almost 100 years, but a number of well-known studies have linked it with cancer in laboratory animals. Today, in the US, foods may contain saccharin, but they are required to carry a warning label pointing out the cancer-causing effects of the substance on laboratory animals. This is just the tip of the low-calorie iceberg.

Dr Jacobson has also called for a US ban on a sweetener known as acesulfame-K, mainly because the CSPI claims that this substance has been inadequately tested. Even the tests that have been conducted show that acesulfame-K causes cancer in animals – which means it may pose a risk for humans. In the UK, government experts admitted that the safety data on acesulfame-K was not ideal, but decided that there was enough evidence to prove its safety anyway – and so it may be found on British supermarket shelves.

Aspartame – found in products such as Nutrasweet® or Canderel® – poses more specific problems. One of its constituents is an amino acid called phenylalanine, and babies born with an illness called phenylketonuria (PKU disease) can't cope with it. Raised levels of phenylalanine may cause brain damage and retardation – which is why products containing aspartame should, by rights, carry a warning label. Many of them do not.

Cyclamates, another artificial sweetening group, were banned in America in 1970, and later in the UK, after tests showed a link with cancer in laboratory animals. Scientists now think that cyclamates increase the potential of other chemicals to cause cancer, yet recent European legislation on sweeteners means cyclamates are again provisionally allowed in the UK.

This appalling lack of common sense has turned shopping into a type of chemical roulette. No healthy person needs extra sugar, let alone artificial chemical sweeteners – particularly when they've no idea such sweeteners are even present in the foods they buy.

GM foods: British retailers' response In the UK, the consumer backlash to GM foods has been vitriolic, and it has raised the whole profile of the anti-GM campaign to such an extent that major retailers and food chains have bowed to public opinion. Iceland was the first multiple store to ban genetically modified foods from its products, then Marks & Spencer announced a total ban on GM foods in all of its stores. While other supermarket chains banned GM products from their own-label food products, most did not insist that manufacturers of branded items remove it from theirs. Because M&S sells only foods bearing the store's own St Michael label, its outlets are, in theory, the only ones whose wares are completely free from any genetic modification.

What has become apparent is that the opposition to genetic modification isn't just a middle-class, muesli-belt fad. Across the nation, people from all walks of life are showing concern. As a result, fast-food chains such as Wimpy, Pizza Express, Burger King, Kentucky Fried Chicken, and Domino's Pizza have all declared intentions to become GM-free zones. The marketing director of Domino's told me this firm wasn't satisfied with assurances from suppliers that included phrases like "subject to availability". Accordingly, Domino's has already instituted a range of its own tests to make sure its products are GM free.

Members of the organic movement have an absolute interdiction against all GM foods, food products or ingredients. They may not be used in any product that is certified organic, or fed to any animal on an organic farm.

sources and further reading

BOOKS

Brostoff, Jonathan and Challacombe, Stephen. **Food Allergy and Intolerance**. London: Bailliere Tindal, 1987.

Carson, Rachel. **Silent Spring**. New York: Houghton Mifflin, 1962. Reprinted 1994.

Macrae, R, Robinson, RK and Sadler, MJ (eds). **Encyclopaedia of Food Science, Food Technology and Nutrition** (8 volumes). London: Academic Press, 1993.

Feingold, Ben. **Why Your Child is Hyperactive**. New York: Random House, 1974.

Hanssen, Maurice. **E for Additives**. Wellingborough: Thorsons Publishing, 1986.

Jacobsen, Michael, et al. **Safe Food**. Los Angeles: Living Planet Press, 1991.

Bernard, RW. **The Organic Way to Health** (series) Pomeroy, Washington, USA: Health Research.

Balfour, Lady Eve and Yellowleas, Walter. **Soil, Food and Health**. London: The Wholefood Trust Ltd.

JOURNALS

Bottom Line Health. PO Box 53408, Boulder, Colorado, USA

The Food Magazine, published by The Food Commission, 94 White Lion Street, London N1 9PF.

Which? Magazine. The Consumers' Association, 2 Marylebone Rd, London NW1 4DF.

Living Earth, the magazine of The Soil Association, Bristol House, 40–56 Victoria Street, Bristol BS1 6BY.

Pesticides News. The Pesticides Trust, 49 Effra Rd, London SW2 1EZ.

Food, Nutrition and the Prevention of Cancer: A Global Perspective. Washington DC: the World Cancer Research Fund and the American Institute for Cancer Research, 1997.

ORGANISATIONS

Center for Science in the Public Interest, Suite 300, 1875 Connecticut Avenue NW, Washington DC, USA.

Friends of the Earth, 26–28 Underwood Street, London N1 7JQ.

The Soil Association, Bristol House, 40–56 Victoria Street, Bristol BS1 6BY.

US Food and Drug Administration (US FDA), Washington DC, USA.

UK Ministry of Agriculture, Fisheries and Food (MAFF), Nobel House, 17 Smith Square, London SW1P 3JR.

WEBSITES

Johns Hopkins Health Information: www.intelihealth.com

Mayo Clinic: www.mayohealth.org

Consumer's Union USA: www.consunion.org/contact

The Soil Association: www.earthfoods.co.uk/soil.whator

PANUPS (Pesticide Action Network Update Service): www.panna.org

glossary

Agrochemicals Chemicals and chemical compounds, including pesticides and fertilisers, that are used in modern intensive-farming methods.

Aldicarb Highly toxic herbicide.

Amino acid Any one of a group of organic compounds that occur naturally in plant and animal tissues and form the basis of proteins.

Antibiotic Substance produced by a micro-organism that is able to inhibit or kill another micro-organism.

Antioxidant Substance that inhibits oxidation. In the body, antioxidants are thought to prevent the destruction of vitamin C, slow the destruction of body cells and strengthen the immune system.

Aspartame Artificial sweetener that is used widely in diet drinks, desserts and branded sugar substitutes. Claims have been made that it is responsible for headaches, blurred vision and hyperactivity, but these have not yet been proven.

Beta-carotene Powerful antioxidant the body transforms into vitamin A.

Biodiversity The rich and natural state of the environment in which a number of different species, both plant and animal, co-exist in ecological balance.

Bioflavonoid (also known as vitamin P) Biologically active flavonoid.

BSE (Bovine spongiform encephalopathy, or "mad cow disease") Slow-progressing, ultimately fatal disease that infects cattle, usually between ages of three to five years. Believed to have arisen when cattle, naturally herbivorous animals, were fed processed offal from sheep infected with a disease called scrapie. Prior to 1988, cows that died from BSE were still processed and put into the food chain. The practice of offal-feeding has since been banned, but there is no way of telling if non-organic cattle are in fact free of the disease. *See also* CJD.

CJD (Creuzfeldt-Jakob Disease) Rapidly progressing form of dementia usually occurring in people aged 40 to 65 which can render them helpless within a year. Since the advent of BSE, instances have appeared in much younger people, and it is believed that it has been transmitted by cattle infected with the BSE virus *(see* BSE). The incubation period of the new strain may be as long as 20 years, so there is no way of knowing how many people are infected.

Capsaicin Colourless, beneficial irritant found in various capsicums, or peppers.

Carotenoid Any one of the various (usually) yellow to red pigments found widely in plants and animals.

Chlorfenapyr Pesticide. Reported to be one of the most toxic to birds.

Coumarin A white substance that beneficially affects blood flow.

DDT Highly toxic pesticide. Stored in fatty tissues, it can cause chronic illness and affects the central nervous system, sometimes resulting in death. Its effects were once thought to be non-toxic to humans, but the opposite has proved to be the case. Consuming animals that have ingested DDT, or eaten other animals that have ingested DDT, will poison any human who eats the meat.

Diazinon Organophosphate pesticide.

Diuretic Any substance that increases the production of urine by the kidneys.

Estragole Volatile oil.

Fatty acid Any of the numerous beneficial fats that occur naturally in fats, waxes and essential oils and are good for the heart.

Folic acid Vitamin of the B complex used to treat nutritional anaemias.

Flavonoid A beneficial phytochemical that tends to occur in plants that are high in vitamin C.

Free radicals Naturally occurring oxygen molecules that damage the body and are thought to play a significant role in the aging process.

Fungicides Poisonous substance used to destroy fungi.

Herbicide Poisonous substance used to destroy unwanted vegetation.

Hydroponics The process of growing plants in sand, gravel or liquid, without natural soil, but with added nutrients.

Insecticide Poisonous substance used to kill undesirable insects.

Limonene Substance that occurs in the essential oils of many citrus fruits.

Linalol Volatile oil.

Lindane Highly toxic insecticide which can cause liver and kidney damage, convulsions, and damage to the central nervous system. Also causes dermatitis, headache and nausea in smaller doses. Disease has been noted in people who have eaten bread contaminated with lindane, as well as in nursing babies whose mothers ate the bread.

Malathion Organophosphate insecticide used widely on non-organic crops, especially fruits and vegetables. Highly toxic, symptoms of poisoning include blurred vision, nosebleeds, nausea and diarrhoea. Closely related to Sarin, a deadly nerve gas, which can kill a person in 15 minutes with only one small drop on the skin.

Metalaxyl Systemic chemical which gets into the bodies of vegetables.

Metaldehyde Anti-slug treatment.

Molluscicide Poisonous substance used to destroy snails, slugs and other invertebrates.

Monocropping Cultivation of a single crop taken from a single strain (of wheat, corn, etc).

Monosodium glutamate Flavour enhancer prevalent in many Chinese foods as well as other processed foods, including stock cubes, tinned meats and packaged and tinned soups.

Mono-unsaturated fat Type of fat believed to offer protection against heart disease and atherosclerosis.

Foods rich in mono-unsaturates include avocados, olive oil and peanuts.

Myalgic Encephalomyelitis (ME) Condition that usually follows a viral infection and involves tiredness, muscle pain, lack of concentration, panic attacks, memory loss and depression.

Nitrates/Nitrites Chemical substances added to fertilisers, pesticides, plastics and various toiletries; it is also used to preserve colours in meats. Believed to cause a number of illnesses in humans, including cancer.

Organic Technically, anything relating to or derived from natural organisms, whether or plant or animal origin. For the purposes of this book, an organic lifestyle is the only sensible one on offer. The word is synonymous with "living", "breathing" and "natural".

Organochlorine Family of pesticides that includes DDT (*see* DDT); chlorinated hydrocarbons.

Organophosphates Family of pesticides that includes malathion and friends (*see* Malathion); phosphorus-containing organic pesticides.

Paraquat Highly toxic herbicide. Poisoning symptoms included liver and kidney damage, abdominal pain, and ulceration of the tongue.

Parathion Nerve gas that is also used as an insecticide. Extremely toxic and fatal to those whose skin comes in contact with it: death results in 30 minutes to 12 hours. While the bulk of poisonings occur in people who have been exposed to sprayed fields, or who have handled vegetables and fruits that have been sprayed, at least two children have died after eating potatoes fried in fat that was contaminated with parathion (*see also* Malathion).

Pesticide Any chemical substance used to kill insects, rodents, weeds and other living "pests". Besides being stored in both plants and animals which may then be eaten by man, pesticides may also be absorbed directly by humans through the skin, through inhalation or by ingestion.

Phenylalanine Amino acid essential for growth in babies and nitrogen metabolism in adults.

Phenylketonuria Disease in which individuals are unable to metabolize the amino acid phenylalanine (*see* above)

Phthalate Acid derived from benzene, often used in pesticides.

Phytochemical Any of the natural chemicals that occur in plants.

Pyrethrum (pyrethrin) Neurotoxic insecticide extracted from chrysanthemums grown in Zaire and Kenya. Large doses result in paralysis and death; small doses in headaches, digestive upsets and loss of feeling in parts of the face.

Salmonella Bacterium that causes food poisoning. In addition to growing in undercooked poultry or cooked foods that have not been properly refrigerated, it is more likely to be found in battery-farmed eggs where it is passed on from unhealthy birds.

Selenium Antioxidant mineral that helps protect tissues against damage from free radicals – which means that it also helps slow the aging process. Brazil nuts are one good source.

Tartrazine E-number additive that is used to enhance colour; thought to have serious effects on food-sensitive individuals (*see* pp 14–15).

Toxin Poisonous substance produced by bacteria.

Triazophos Organophosphate.

index

author's note

I would like to thank, once again, my commissioning editor at Mitchell Beazley, Margaret Little, for her many ideas and fantastic support. And Jamie Ambrose, who remained undaunted and uncomplaining throughout the writing and editing of this book. Tracy Killick and Miranda Harvey for working above and beyond the call of duty to make the book look as good as it does. My secretary, Janet, whose tireless help in this matter was, as it is in all others, greatly and sincerely appreciated. And, of course, my constant support and now, happily, my wife, Sally.

Michael van Straten